What People Are Sa

...Mind blown! What insights will speak to you?"

"Gary Wilbers has some wonderful gems to live by in his latest book. The insight that woke me up was to live by a compass rather than by the clock. Mind blown. What insights will speak to you?"

-Scott Wilhite, Best-selling Author of
The 7 Core Skills of Everyday Happiness

"...guaranteed to make a positive impact on everyone..."

"GREAT job. This book is guaranteed to make a positive impact on everyone who reads it and a greater positive change in their life if they implement even a fraction of your guidance. It has for me."

-Mark Ricca, Business Consultant, Trainer,
Coach, Keynote Speaker

"...I CHOOSE to have a great attitude."

"Positivity in life matters greatly. It is what helps drive change in myself and others. This book helped me realize that I can be much more positive. I choose to have a great attitude."

-Matt Ward, Breakthrough Champion

"...Really touched our hearts and gave us a boost in our journey..."

"Your book is incredible. Really touched our hearts and gave us a boost in our journey. We read it through in a couple of hours and are going to reread and take notes. What a gift!"

-Jude & Mary Markway

"…Gary has provided practical ways to put each of his lessons into action in your daily life…"

"In Cultivate Positive Culture, *Gary Wilbers has provided a powerful set of lessons in an easy to read, easy to follow, and positive story that everyone should enjoy. I found myself identifying with many of the lessons learned by the main character, Lloyd, especially regarding "forgiveness." After reading this particular lesson, and how Lloyd was able to use it to move to a better place in his life, I felt inspired and empowered to show forgiveness towards someone in my own life that I needed to forgive. How freeing doing just this one thing has made me feel! In "Part 2" of the book, Gary has provided practical ways to put each of his lessons into action in your daily life. They were so well done that I look forward to sharing this book with my teenage daughters so they can start implementing Gary's 10 Daily Actions into their lives right away!"*

-Daran Wastchak, DaranWastchak.com

"…Gary is an excellent mentor to those hoping to grow and improve as leaders in life."

I enjoyed reading and living Gary's 10 daily actions to faithful living. This is a great reminder to me of the positive, optimistic, energetic, enthusiastic, faith-filled, and loving person Gary Wilbers truly is. He is able to teach these ten actions because he actually lives these ten actions. He walks the talk and leads by example. He is a great role model in his personal and professional life. Gary is an excellent mentor to those hoping to grow and improve as leaders in life.

-Didier Aur, Principal at Saint Ann Catholic School

"...has helped my health, spirituality, relationships, self and family living..."

"Taking the time to read Cultivating Positive Culture - 10 Actions to Faithful Living *has helped my Health, Spirituality, Relationships, Self and Family Living. I guarantee it will ignite yours as well! We all have a Scott and Lloyd in our lives!* God Love ya and see you all at the TOP like Lloyd in this book."

-Eddie Mulholland, Market Director at Vitae Foundation

...Not only is this book much needed in today's environment, but it was much needed in my life."

"My personal takeaway was things don't happen on your timeline; they happen on His. However you're not in the right mindset to receive what He has in store for you, you'll miss it every time. Not only is this book much needed today's environment, but it was much needed in my life."

-Rick Fessler, CH&M Holdings, Inc.

"...brief, enjoyable read sure to create not only positive, but lasting impact."

"Gary Wilbers' new book is informed by his deeply held Christian faith, but regardless of whether you share that faith, there is undeniable value in applying the actions he recommends to your life. As he has before, Gary shares a story in the first part of the book to draw people into the challenges and opportunities that permeate all of our lives. This provides a human backdrop and context for the practical suggestions he offers for application in part two. Cultivate Positive Culture *is a brief, enjoyable read sure to create not only positive, but lasting impact."*

Jeff Cobb, Co-founder and Managing Director of Tagoras

"I am confident that this book will enrich your life."

"Gary is a man who is authentically driven to bring forth the God given gifts, which each of us has been given. We are blessed to have a man of Gary's caliber championing the causes of faith and family, which ultimately leads to building a positive culture... I am confident that this book will enrich your life".

-Fr. Anthony Viviano

"...I highly recommend that you read this book to unlock your full potential."

Cultivate Positive Culture *is an outstanding book that delivers a powerful spiritual message of how to discover God's purpose for your life. This beautifully written story is one that all readers can relate to and learn from. After reading this book, I am going to be more intentional about incorporating the 10 Actions to Faithful Living to completely transform my life and share my God given gifts with the world. No matter where you are in your spiritual journey, I highly recommend that you read this book to unlock your full potential."*

-Derrich Phillips, Author of *Poverty Powerball*

"I can't wait to apply these foundational principles to my business and more importantly, my life!"

"Everyone needs to get a copy of this book! The principles that Gary shares around building a positive culture are essential. I can't wait to apply these foundational principles to my business and more importantly, my life!

-Alex Demczak, Author of *Thrive U,*
Former SEC Quarterback

CULTIVATE POSITIVE CULTURE

10 Actions to Faithful Living

GARY WILBERS

Published by Business Innovation Group, LLC

Cultivate Positive Culture
10 Actions to Faithful Living
Gary Wilbers
Business Innovation Group, LLC

Published by Business Innovation Group, LLC, Jefferson City, MO

Copyright ©2020 Gary Wilbers

All rights reserved.

Editor: Peggy Luebbert

Cover Design: Aaron Wilbers Studio, LLC

Interior Design: Davis Creative, DavisCreative.com

Library of Congress Cataloging-in-Publication Data

Library of Congress Control Number: 2020916407

Gary Wilbers

Cultivate Positive Culture: *10 Actions to Faithful Living*

ISBN: 978-1-7354307-0-6

Library of Congress subject headings:

1. SEL021000   SELF-HELP / Motivational & Inspirational
    2. BUS106000   BUSINESS & ECONOMICS / Mentoring & Coaching
    3. OCC019000   BODY, MIND & SPIRIT / Inspiration & Personal Growth

2020

Dedication

This book is dedicated to my three children: Chris, Adam and Elle. Each is unique and has brought so much happiness, fun, and joy to Dana's and my lives. You three have given us a purpose beyond our greatest expectations. My hope is that each of you please read this book. (You know sometimes when Dad suggests something, the kids don't always want to listen.)

By sharing this story and the insights I have gained over my fifty-three years of living, I hope to provide a roadmap for you to decide the journey you each want to take in life. Remember: God is good, and you are an instrument for living your life with a purpose and mission. My prayer for each of you is that you choose to live your life with action to fulfill your God-given talents.

Chris, you are our first born. You brought a newness into our lives that we had never experienced before. You are always curious about trying new things and willing to explore. I hope your life continues to be an adventure. Move forward each day and share the gifts you have been given with those who need them.

Adam, you are our active child. You have a big heart and enjoy sports, hunting, and hiking. You are a competitor, but after the competition you just like to enjoy your friends and family. Continue to learn, grow, and become the person God created you to be.

Elle, you are the daughter we prayed for. We were so excited when you came into our family. You strive to reach your goals and work hard to meet your own expectations. Shoot for the stars and achieve your dreams. Keep God in your life and let Him help guide you on your path.

Table of Contents

Acknowledgements

The challenge of writing a book does not lie just with the author. It takes many willing hands to make it a reality. I am a very creative individual, but without the help of others, this book would have never been published. It is with a deep gratitude that I thank these individuals for their efforts in helping me make this dream come true:

Dana, my spouse, life and business partner who thinks I am crazy (sometimes) but always supports me in everything I do. You have such a servant heart, and I can't thank you enough for your guidance, support, and help in creating this book. I appreciate and love you very much.

Peggy, you have been an inspiration since I met you my freshman year in high school. I appreciate you editing this book and sharing your insights about how to make it better. I can't thank you enough for your friendship, and who knew when I was just a freshman, you would be one of my mentors. Words cannot express how I feel. You have been a true blessing to me. Thank you!

Matt Luadzers, you were a great resource who took my concepts and stories and helped me create a first-class fable to inspire our readers. We started our relationship through your aid in updating our website and continued with your collaboration on this book. Thank you for assisting me turn my thoughts, notes, and ideas into a book that helps others change their lives.

Cathy Davis and Davis Creative team, thank you for your support in getting this book published. Your valuable guidance during this process helped make this book a success.

Introduction

This book has been a lifelong journey for me. After reflection and thought I have realized that my life has not been about a destination but about the journey. If you remember the story of Jesus' life here on earth, He was not waiting for the destination. He was creating a journey and helping all that came in contact with Him to live their life for a greater purpose.

As you read this book, my prayer is that you will reflect where you are on your journey in life. We all need to continue moving forward and living our life with faith. The first part of this book is Lloyd's journey and his struggles to understand his purpose. This story illustrates and helps us to understand that we each have struggles, obstacles, and challenges which help us become who we were meant to be. Think back to the stories in the Bible. God did not call the most uprighteous disciples to follow Him and build the church's foundation. He called people like you and me to become the person He created us to be.

The second part of the book takes the 10 Actions from the story and gives you a roadmap for implementing these daily actions into your life. Throughout my lifetime I have discovered these 10 Actions help draw me closer to who I need to be. I strive to implement them into my daily living. Don't try to implement them all immediately. Begin with the action(s) that impacts you, your family, friends, co-workers, etc. This will move you closer to the person God created you to be.

My hope is that this book will help you on your journey as you continue to search for who you were meant to be.

"Your purpose defines you, guides you, and allows you to be the person God created you to be."

Make it a GREAT day!

-Gary Wilbers

Part 1

The Accident

Panicked and nearly weeping, he stood over the body as it lay stretched out before him. A cold sweat formed on his brow. Blood trickled toward his boot. As he lifted his leg to step away from the stream of maroon, the memory of what had just occurred flashed like lightning back into his mind.

He turned quickly and over his left shoulder yelled, "Is everyone alright?"

"We're okay," came back a shaken voice. The family emerged from the vehicle currently parked half in and half out of the ditch and shoulder. They walked closer to Lloyd and the body near him. After crossing the two-lane road, the stranger stuck out his hand. "Hi, I'm Tim."

"Hey, Tim, I'm Lloyd. We've got quite a situation here, don't we?"

"Yes, we do, Lloyd." Tim's mouth was shaped in such a way that it looked as if he was going to speak but hadn't quite figured out what to say.

"I think you clipped my truck trying to avoid this," Lloyd said as he nodded his head toward the front of the semi. Lloyd could hear the unmistakable sound of retching behind him as the smallest of the four standing nearby emptied a nervous, disgusted stomach onto the asphalt a few feet away.

"She'll be okay. We need to exchange insurance information and deal with this," said Tim as he pointed to the ground where the body lay.

April, the smallest from the family involved in the accident, wiped her mouth with a towel her mother had handed her. She approached her father and Lloyd with curious caution. "I've never seen a dead body before," said April. "Where is the other half?"

"The rest of him is toward the front of my truck," said Lloyd as he glanced toward the cab. He could see blood splattered down his trailer.

"Let's get him off the road," said Tim. Lloyd agreed with a simple head nod.

"I will get a tarp and the rest of him," said Lloyd.

"We should bury him," said April. A silent agreement was made to haul the deer carcass back just beyond the edge of the forest and create a shallow grave.

"It's a good thing you have a shovel and tarp for this. It will make it easier. There sure aren't a lot of cars on this road, are there?" said Tim.

Lloyd watched how the yellow, flashing hazard lights from both the car and his semi contrasted against the near dusk, mountain-view sky. With nighttime getting close, Lloyd and Tim both knew they had to accomplish a lot in a short time.

Lloyd quickly dug a shallow grave to place both halves in knowing that later that night some lucky, scavenging wildlife would come sniffing around for an easy meal. His hope was that they had moved it back far enough that the other wildlife would not be in danger from any passersby.

"Can we say a small prayer?" April said as she made her way through the small thicket of the forest edge.

"Sure we can, April," Tim said.

Everyone bowed their heads to ask the Creator to bless this graceful animal with peace. Lloyd, however, lowered his head but popped it back up after he observed everyone else's eyes were closed. His prayer was just as nonexistent as his head bowing. Lloyd stood silently waiting until he heard the

Amen. He then looked down and quickly raised his head to meet Tim and April.

"Should we call the local authorities to make a report, Tim?" asked Lloyd.

"No, I don't see much point in doing that. I'm just going to take you for being an honest man since you haven't hesitated about anything out here this evening. It's getting dark though, and I need to somehow get my car out of that ditch."

"That ditch shouldn't be a problem. I have a tow chain in the back behind the sleeper. We'll get you hooked up and out of there in no time," said Lloyd.

Lloyd walked around the front of the semi where he noticed that it wasn't Tim's car that had clipped him but a piece of antler. Lloyd pried it out, stuffed it in his pocket, inspected the damage, and retrieved the tow chain. They worked together to hook Tim's car to the tow chain and the semi. Lloyd climbed back in the truck and sparked the engine to life. Tim returned to his vehicle and prepared to be pulled from the ditch. Lloyd found the low gear, applied a little diesel to the churning engine, and everything started moving.

With the car back on the road, Tim and Lloyd shook hands in preparation to go their separate ways. Tim suggested to Lloyd it would be a good idea to exchange phone numbers. Lloyd reached into his pocket to retrieve his pen. Touching his fingers to the antler piece reminded him that he wanted to give it to Tim. "Hey, before you go, I found this in the grill. It wasn't your car after all. Keep it if you want. Maybe someday you can use it for a knife or something."

"Thanks," Tim said taking the antler piece. They turned and went their separate ways.

Lloyd arrived at the depot the next day. He and his work friends found it miserable since Ryan, who was brash and impulsive, had become the supervisor over four years ago. In the eighteen years working at Forward Trucking Inc., Lloyd had never witnessed so much turnover as in the past five.

As he pulled into the yard of the complex, his phone was buzzing and flashing with a regional alert about a white male who had gone missing in the area he had just been. "Last seen, huh, that's right near where we met that poor deer," he said out loud to no one.

"Hey, Lloyd, did you get that run done?" asked Ryan as Lloyd walked through the depot station office to drop off expenses and file his shipping report completing the run so that it could be added to the pay period.

"I did, Ryan," Lloyd confirmed.

"Took a little longer than usual for you this time," said Ryan as he peered over his glasses like an elementary teacher preparing to scold a student.

"Maybe just a little," Lloyd replied. He was distracted by the television behind Ryan. A news team was broadcasting about the man that Lloyd had gotten the alert about.

"Looks like someone got himself into trouble," said Ryan. "You're due back out in the morning, so go home and get some rest."

"I just got back from a run. I need to spend some time with my family, Ryan."

"Do you want to waste time or feed that family? It's your choice, Lloyd."

Lloyd glared at Ryan after the exchange but knew there was no reasoning with this kind of overbearing behavior. He recalled how Ryan had brashly slashed several other co-workers' jobs at the snap of a fiery finger. Lloyd turned, left the building, and headed home.

"Dad's home!" his excited daughter shouted to the rest of the family. He got out of his car leaving everything else behind except for the fact that tomorrow he would have to leave again.

"I have to get back on the road in the morning," Lloyd told Liz.

"What? Lloyd, you just got home," Liz stated with disapproval. "If we didn't need the money your job brings in so badly, I would tell you to call and quit today, but as it is, we are only two paychecks away from losing everything we have worked so hard to build."

"I know. I don't know what else to do, Liz. It's the only thing I've ever really done and starting over just...well, you know what that looks like," he said disappointedly.

"Let's enjoy our time together, Lloyd," Liz reluctantly said accepting the fact that she would spend even more time without her husband.

Lloyd rose in the morning and quietly got ready to leave. He lovingly kissed his wife goodbye whispering, "I love you, Elizabeth." Touching her soft hair, he left for the rough road. His order and trailer number assignment were in his box at the depot. Lloyd went through all the steps to get himself started on another long trip yet again pulling him away from the ones he loved.

The Message

"Hello," Lloyd said confused as to why Ryan was calling him knowing he was in the beginning of his haul.

"Lloyd, it's Ryan. This is your last run with this company. Turn in your ID badge and keys when you get back. I know what you were up to on the last run, Buddy. You're going to jail. I found the tarp and the shovel with dirt on it. I'm calling the police today. You killed that guy, didn't you, you idiot?"

"Wait a d…"

Ryan cut him off. "Don't explain this to me. The boys in blue will be all ears." With a slam of the phone, Ryan abruptly ended the call.

Lloyd, upset and needing to talk, reached for his CB radio and using his handle Teddy Bear called for any truckers that might be in hearing distance.

A voice came through the speaker of the square device and said, "Come on back, Teddy Bear. "

Lloyd explained everything that had just taken place. As Lloyd viewed the on-ramp of nearby traffic entering the interstate, he noticed a white truck preparing to merge. As the truck entered the highway, Lloyd noticed the trailer had a unique design on the back. At the bottom, was an arching line that looked like a hill. Under the hill were the words "My Life is a Message." "Hmm, what the heck does that mean?" said Lloyd.

Suddenly the semi's cab was filled with a smooth, calming voice coming from the CB radio. "Hey, this is Scott. I'm trying to reach Teddy Bear. Come back, Teddy Bear."

Lloyd grabbed the CB radio microphone. "This is Teddy Bear, come back."

"Teddy Bear, I heard part of your story as you were coming up the interstate. I was thumbing through the channels when I heard you telling your story. I stopped and listened to the rest. I don't use a handle. I'm just Scott P. Meyer out here. You can identify me easily. My trailer has a unique design on it. It has a cross on top of a hill and a short message under it."

"I saw you pull on the interstate. I'm just a short distance behind you," Lloyd replied.

"I would like to invite you to lunch. Know any places good along this route?"

Lloyd's eyes focused in the distance. His mind went along many miles of the run remembering the good spots. "Umm, sure. Okay. You sure you want to do that? I mean we don't know each other at all."

Silence. Then again, the cab was filled with the calming voice that reassured Lloyd. "Yes, of course."

"Okay, how about Chopping Block? It's a BBQ place, and I always stop there on this route."

"Sounds good. I will see you there."

The wheels turning and singing that rhythmic song of tread humming on the pavement put Lloyd deep in thought. After driving for some time, Chopping Block was in view.

Lloyd picked up the transmitter. "Come back, Scott. This is Teddy Bear."

"Scott here."

"How will I recognize you, Scott?"

"You'll notice the back of my shirt matches the tail of my trailer. I will be waiting for you."

Lloyd reached the restaurant parking lot and parked his semi. Sitting in silence for a moment, Lloyd contemplated why this stranger wanted to meet him for a meal. He took his phone from his pocket and sent a text to Liz. "Hey, Liz, I got invited to eat with another truck driver. Not sure who he is. Going to find out though. At Chopping Block now. I will text you when I get back to the truck."

Lloyd climbed out of the truck, walked across the pavement, and entered the restaurant. He quickly identified Scott by the shirt he was wearing. Lloyd cautiously approached Scott and tapped him on the shoulder.

Scott turned with a bright smile on his face and that calm voice Lloyd heard on the CB radio said, "Hi, I'm Scott." He and Lloyd shook hands as Lloyd said, "I'm Lloyd."

The hostess escorted both men to a seat. After being seated across from one another, Scott wasted no time explaining the reason for the meeting. "Lloyd, I heard a lot of what you said today. I want you to know I don't believe what Ryan is doing is right or totally legal."

"I didn't do any...," said Lloyd feeling as though he was on trial.

"I know. I could hear the outrage in your voice at the audacity of Ryan's accusations." That sentence rang in Lloyd's head, and he thought to himself that this isn't some random truck driver.

"There is something I would like to share with you." Scott unrolled a paper napkin and then withdrew a pen from his shirt pocket.

As he began to draw, the shape of a half box appeared on the top portion of the napkin. Scott wrote the word "Income" at the top of the partial box and then moved to the middle where he wrote "Family." Finally, moving to the side of the bottom line, he wrote "Charity."

Lloyd, sitting transfixed in thought, watched curiously as Scott finished the last mark of the arrow at both ends of the half box. Scott then drew a line through the center going up and added two more marks at the end making it an ascending arrow.

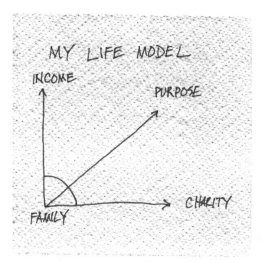

Scott looked up from the napkin at Lloyd. The same calm manner of speaking that Lloyd was quickly becoming accustomed to found its way to his ears again.

"You see as I heard you speaking today, I wondered to myself where things fit in your life. I heard the fears in your voice. I thought perhaps the smallest thing I could do for you this afternoon is to buy your lunch, and the biggest, most memorable thing I could do for you is to share a simple napkin drawing. Are you in for that?"

"Yes, I believe so," Lloyd said in a cautious tone.

"Good. I will keep going. I read a book awhile back called <u>Positive Culture Wins</u>. It changed me for the better. The author goes into detail about creating a positive culture in business, life, or both. I took the message to heart. As I heard you recreating the interaction you had with Ryan, I realized that you were similar to the person I was in my past. Not that we are the same person or have the same set of circumstances, but that you have a desperation judging by the sound in your voice. What I heard was a man that is led by his heart. A man that is desperate for something new, something rewarding, and something that doesn't include the frustration you face in your day-to-day life."

"I...I...don't know," said Lloyd bewildered and astonished at this stranger's perceptibility.

"The message on the back of my trailer and my shirt wasn't by accident. It was inspired by a thought in that book. After I began creating habits around my real goals every day, it occurred to me very plainly what was good in my life and what wasn't. My motto became "My Life is a Message," but there is more to it than that."

Looking back down at his napkin drawing, Scott began by pointing his pen at the drawing. "The arrow in the center is 'Purpose,' but you can call it something else if you want. I will explain all of this to you further, but only if you are interested."

"I am very interested. I really want to hear what you have to say. You've piqued my interest with what you have said already."

"Great! I am so glad you are willing."

Scott was suddenly interrupted by the ringing cell phone in Lloyd's front pocket. Lloyd examined the brightly lit screen of the device as the number displayed itself. "I'm sorry, Scott. I have to take this."

"Hello, this is Lloyd."

"Hello, Lloyd, this is Officer Jefferies of the Utah State Highway Patrol. We received an anonymous tip regarding a homicide we are investigating."

Lloyd's face was becoming red and visibly contorted as the stress mounted from head to toe. Scott was observing the change in Lloyd's demeanor as the phone call continued.

"Lloyd, we have contacted the state patrol in your home state. You can either discuss this over the phone now, or when you return from your haul, you can go into the highway patrol office closest to you. We need to ask you a few questions. If you refuse to voluntarily report to that office, a warrant will be issued."

"I understand, but I...I don't have anything to do with this case."

"Either way, Sir, we have to clear you from any wrongdoing once a report is made of this nature."

Lloyd angrily said goodbye to the officer and abruptly ended the call. Looking up, Lloyd saw Scott staring directly at him.

"Lloyd, I know you are angry right now, but this is the perfect opportunity to explain more to you."

"It's Ryan. I just know it's him. I'm gonna..."

Scott interrupted abruptly, "Is your life a message? If you say it is, then what message are you sending right now? You are allowing this to control you, your thoughts, and your physical presence. This goes well beyond if you are guilty or innocent. This is now a training ground full of snares, wires, and pitfalls. It's how you navigate this training ground that will determine your future, but you are currently living in the past."

"Scott, this just happened," said Lloyd as his face returned to the brighter shade of red it was previously.

Both men sat in uncomfortable silence.

Slowly Scott began speaking, "You need to understand that you have to take responsibility for yourself." Scott drew his breath in deeply, held it for a few seconds, and exhaled slowly. Scott left silence between his words in acknowledgment of their brevity and also to allow them to permeate throughout Lloyd's mind. "This will only get as difficult as you make it. Let's make a goal right now to get through this rough patch."

"Okay. I'm sorry...I am just...so..." Lloyd looked up and away. A tear gently welled up in the corner of his eye. "It's not just this thing with Ryan, and the police, and the questioning. I'm innocent. I didn't do anything to anyone. These things just keep coming up. One thing after another."

"Good. This is good. You recognize that things are not the way you want them to be. Right, Lloyd?"

"Yes."

"Your life is a message that you can make whatever you want it to be. That's done from the very beginning of your thought process. You have a choice. You can let this control you, or you can take control. I strongly believe and am living proof that you get in life what you create. You get what you expect and what you think turns into what you expect. This conversation you have with yourself and those thoughts that filter through your being become your true reality. They become the new you. Being proactive in your thoughts, deeds, and words will drive your expectations to new highs."

"I've never known how to do that. My childhood was rough. My teens were rougher. Man, it's just been a battle my whole life to this point and now this nonsense with Ryan and the police."

"Lloyd," Scott paused reflecting deeply. The sounds of dishes clanking, orders being taken, and footsteps of some as they made their way to the salad bar became noticeable. "I just want to make clear what I'm saying this afternoon. It's not advice. It's about the future you create, and the culture you create it in."

"Hi, what will you have today?" came a bright, cheerful question from the waitress.

They ordered their meals. Shortly after, the hot, steaming plates of deliciousness arrived. Lloyd took his fork and speared the first bite. Before he could lift the fork to his mouth, Scott interrupted, "May I bless this food before we eat?"

"Sure, Scott. I'm sorry about that. It's not something I do regularly."

Scott immediately went into prayer blessing the food. At first, Lloyd pretended to pray and then lifted his head to watch Scott in deep reverence. "Amen," the two men said aloud. They picked up their forks and began eating as Lloyd thought about Scott's previous words.

Scott finished his last bite, sipped his water for a moment, and then asked very directly, "Do you take responsibility for your own life?"

"I guess I do, but some of this is way beyond my control."

"I know it seems that way, Lloyd. After all, you aren't in charge of the reactions and actions of other people. You are in charge of your actions and your reactions. Lloyd, are you a person of action?"

"I would like to think I am."

"What do you want in your life?"

"Right now, I just want to be happy."

"A lot of unhappy people say that and are presently still unhappy. Are you a man of action or not?"

"I guess it depends. I have been rather lazy with my career, and I guess with my marriage considering the impact my career has had on it. Thinking that question all the way through, I suppose I have been a person of inaction most of my adult life. I have kept my head down and nose to the grindstone, as they say."

"Lloyd, my new friend, we are going to have a great opportunity together watching you grow from where you are today to a new identity. You will become a positive culture creating, energy-producing, and successful being. You will become the person you have always wanted to be."

"How is everything?" the waitress had silently appeared beside the table.

"Everything is wonderful," Scott replied with a smile.

"Great. I will get your check."

"Before she returns, I want to ask you a very sensitive question: How is your spiritual walk? Take your time with that one. If you don't want to answer right now, that's okay. Sometimes we all need a little time to figure out exactly where we are."

"Well, I can tell you that I'm not walking, running, or crawling spiritually. I haven't even considered God in my future and barely in my past," Lloyd said in nearly a whisper as he felt embarrassed.

"Lloyd, I'm not a judging kind of guy. That's not my role here on earth. I also know that not everyone has faith or belief in something greater. I try to share my faith with as many people as I can. I think it's important to, at the very least, have that discussion. I have settled on the idea that wisdom in one's life comes from the same well as faith. To be faithful to the Creator and to ourselves, we allow our experiences to mold us. We learn from them and grow every day. After all, if we aren't growing, we are retracting. What a waste that is!"

"What about the people such as the agnostics or faithless who don't believe?"

"That is a really good question. The fact is we are all created. We all have an accountability for the life we have. Even if that life has been difficult or the struggles have been numerous and challenging, we are accountable. We should all use the wisdom we possess to enrich and reward ourselves in education, leadership, faith, and health. Recognizing that we have wisdom opens the path to attaining the knowledge we need to be whatever we want."

"Well, I can tell you I never set my mind to be a truck driver. It just happened. I have these thoughts about how the industry could run smoother, better, and more efficiently."

"Here you go." The bright, cheery voice of the waitress returned.

Scott took the ticket quickly not allowing Lloyd the opportunity to offer to pay for the meal the two shared. Lloyd watched as Scott tallied the bill with a $50.00 tip! "Here is my card, Lloyd. I expect we will be very good friends. I guess we better get back on the road."

"You didn't have to pay for my meal, but I do appreciate it. I have a lot to think about after our conversation. No one has ever taken the time for me like you did today except maybe my wife."

The two men stood, shook hands, said goodbye, and left the table walking away in opposite directions having parked near different doors of the restaurant.

Guilty

As Lloyd approached his truck across the parking lot, he could see the back of Scott's trailer heading out on the highway. That sign gave him such an encouraging feeling as though things were finally looking up. Making a very valuable acquaintance with Scott might be a missing piece in the puzzle of his life. I've never really had a mentor thought Lloyd as he walked to where the truck was sitting, gleaming from being freshly washed at the depot.

Suddenly from nowhere, the descent was upon him. Deafening screams of sirens and shouting of men came from multiple directions. He found many barrels pointed at him. The light of the day was fading. Lloyd noticed it had taken an aggressive glow about it as the surreal began unfolding.

"Get down!" was being shouted over and over. Lloyd complied by lying face down on the warm pavement placing his hands palm down to the back of his head. The moment brought terror. Lloyd could hear running boots and swishing pants as the officers came closer. A knee was placed firmly and directly in his back. Pain shot through his body.

"Cuffs," the officer now nearly sitting on Lloyd yelled. Lloyd heard the clinking of the cuffs as they were transferred from one officer to the other and then the slide of the steel rail locking into its slot. The officer stood Lloyd to his feet and walked him to the waiting SUV.

The room was lit by stagnant fluorescent. It was an interior room with no windows. The walls were bare, and the floor was carpeted but dirty. Lloyd thought that at one time this must have been a file room because the lines from the cabinets were still on the floor. An electromagnetic lock released its grip on the only door. The door opened, and the officer that was on Lloyd's back entered the room. He walked across the seasoned carpet and took a seat across from Lloyd.

"I'm Detective Bernstein. You have been apprehended for questioning after we received an anonymous tip. We understand that you were asked to report to your local highway patrol station. Given the nature of this situation, we couldn't take any chances that you would run. The evidence suggests that you are the person we are looking for. We further understand that you were bragging about this to a coworker."

Suddenly everything happening to Lloyd made sense. In one moment he could see how these events were all related, and exactly why he was sitting in this room.

"We understand that you washed your truck right after you returned to the depot. We contacted your HR department to get a concise idea of what was standard operating procedure. We fully understand washing was within those parameters. We found some tissue and some hair in the grill of your truck that were sent to the lab with a rush order. We will know more soon. Would you like to say anything or have a confession you would like to offer?"

"No. In fact, the truth will come out soon. Do I get a call to contact my lawyer?"

"Yes, when we have completed our questioning."

"No, Detective, I believe that call should happen before."

"Very well then." Looking to his subordinate officer, Detective Bernstein instructed him to allow one phone call.

Shortly after, the officer retrieved a landline telephone with a long cable stretched across the file cabinet tracings. Lloyd requested the card that was in his belongings. The officer left and retrieved it. As the officer handed the card to him, Lloyd abruptly grabbed it. He felt its exterior. Two cards were clung together by static electricity. As he pulled them apart, Tim's card was revealed.

"My alibi," Lloyd murmured. He took the other card, carefully read the number, and dialed the phone.

Innocent

"Hello, this is Scott," came the very quick answer in response to the ringing phone.

"Scott, this is Lloyd."

"Why did the caller ID display highway patrol, Lloyd?"

"Scott, they arrested me and brought me in for questioning. This entire experience is awful. It turns out that snake of man Ryan gave them a tip...a false tip, but he made it. Now I'm here for questioning. I don't have a lawyer, and I don't want to get my wife involved yet if I can help it. I requested them to bring your card, and I called you instead. Is there a way you can come back and help me? They have impounded my truck, and I have no idea what to do."

"Have you said anything at all to the people investigating this?"

"No, not really."

"You should tell them the truth."

"When I get out of this, I'm going to hurt Ryan. I'm going to hurt him so terribly bad."

"It's understandable you would want to do that. We can talk more about that when I get there."

"I'm so sorry to drag you into any of this, but I'm really glad I met you. There is a certain peace about you that brings me calmness."

"I appreciate you saying that. My life is about loving and helping others. My heart is content to be caring. Try to stay calm. We will talk soon."

With that, the two hung up. Anger had taken over Lloyd's mind. He felt his pulse quickening. Looking the officer right in the eyes, Lloyd said, "You go find that detective. I've got something to say to him."

The officer grabbed the phone and left the room. The detective reentered the room swiftly and said, "Lloyd, you have something to tell us?"

"Yes, I'M INNOCENT, and this is freaking ridiculous!"

"Sir, you need to remain calm."

"I will have to remain free of these charges. What do you have on me anyway? Nothing. What happens when you get that hair sample back and find out that it's not human?"

"We will cross that bridge if and when it happens, Sir."

Silence filled the room. No one was talking. Suddenly the phone rang and startled Lloyd who slightly jumped. Answering the phone, Detective Bernstein said, "Yes, this is the detective in charge. Oh, so it's a positive match for a male. Uh-huh and you are sure about that? Very well then, thank you."

The detective put the phone on the cradle and began explaining, "The hair that was found is a match for a male; however, the male, in this case, is a whitetail deer. That means I can no longer hold you here, but it does not clear your name from being a suspect."

"You people with your badges and hunches thought I was guilty all because one person made a false testimony. I was with someone when I presume the deer that I hit left remnants of himself on my truck." Flipping Tim's card onto the table, Lloyd said, "Here! Call that guy!"

"Officer, will you please release the handcuffs from this gentleman? Sir, your truck will remain impounded until we are able to settle this matter. For now, you are free to go."

Lloyd was released from the restraints. He viewed the marks on his wrists rubbing their indentations. For the first time in a long time, he considered God in his business. Perhaps not the business he wanted, but the business at hand. Lloyd followed his escort through the building until he reached the outer exterior door. The thought crossed his mind that he had no option for leaving. Rage and revenge once again occupied his thought process. "This is going to ruin me even though I'm innocent. I can't afford a lawyer. I can barely afford the extra money it's going to cost to stay in this state until they get some answers," he said out loud to himself.

Forgiveness

Lloyd looked up hearing the call of his name. Scott was waving from across the parking lot. The relief of one friend in the world that believed in him swept over Lloyd, and the simple gesture of a wave nearly brought him to tears.

"Hey, Lloyd, it's all going to be okay," Scott said and then smiled warmly as he patted Lloyd on the shoulder. "What you need is a little faith." Scott and Lloyd walked back to Scott's truck. "Climb on in."

Shutting the cabin doors, the two men settled in their seats. "I know we haven't known each other long, Scott, but this is about the lowest I've ever been."

"Did you do what they are accusing you of doing?"

"No, I thought you…"

"Lloyd, calm down. I knew the answer. If I thought you were capable of doing some atrocious action like that, I wouldn't have turned around to be here right now."

"Why are you here?"

"I'm here because you need a friend. I'm sure all the things I said at the restaurant are still somewhat fresh in your mind. I'm going to impart a revolutionary idea."

"Oh yeah? What is that?"

"Forgiveness."

The silence that fell in the truck was deafening as the idea muted Lloyd. Anger welled up in him once more.

"WHY...HOW...I CAN'T...," Lloyd burst forth. "Why are you telling me to forgive Ryan?"

"Look, I know it's unusual in our time to hear this kind of truth or idea. I came back because I care. Remember me saying that my life is about loving and doing my best to help people. I strive every day to make people and things flourish. It's governed by the amount of time, care, and energy I give to those people and things. Today I'm giving that care and energy to you. I want to see you flourish, but you won't be able to do that until you release this angry energy. You won't be able to let the future you want happen until you stop feeding this negative energy. Negativity hampers your positive thoughts and hopes. You are left with anger, resentment, and vengefulness. Those will destroy your soul and spirit. Forgiving does not mean that the other guy... what's his name?"

"Ryan"

"It doesn't mean that Ryan won't face a penalty for his actions. I believe in you, and soon there will be reconciliation for your innocence."

"How do I even start? I have so much raw emotion pointed right at that stupid face of his. I don't know if now is the right time."

"This is exactly the right time. Imagine what overcoming these strong feelings will do to the root of this forgiveness. Those roots will bury and grow deep leaving you with a feeling of peace."

"How do I start, Scott?"

"Will you pray with me? I don't mean what you did at the restaurant. I mean really pray?"

Lloyd felt the heat of embarrassment cross his face. He wondered as he stared out the window of Scott's truck how he knew. "Ok, Scott, lead the way. I am truly at the end of myself with all of this."

Scott quietly opened with reverent prayer. As he prayed for the situation, a few revealing things about himself were disclosed. "Amen," Scott announced.

"Amen," Lloyd said.

"Can you speak the words out loud now, Lloyd?"

"I still can't, Scott."

"Forget about everything else and focus on this one thing. Focus on what your life can become. If you let this go, imagine the things you could do for others. Imagine how much your life could flourish. I wasn't always on this faith walk. I told you that you reminded me a lot of my past self. The situations are different, but the attitude is the same. Forgiveness was the best and truly the most difficult thing I have ever done. Once I accepted that forgiveness both to myself and others, I was truly free of any shred of anger."

"Give me a little time, and I might be able to. I just cannot forgive him now. It's too much like putting the square peg in the round hole. It just isn't fitting at the moment," Lloyd said sighing heavily and gazing out the windshield.

Attitude

"Lloyd, Lloyd, it's time to wake up," said Scott while shaking Lloyd.

"Morning, Scott," Lloyd said wearily as the lack of comfort through the night began to appear in aching joint form.

"Morning, Lloyd. How did you sleep?"

"Fine. It took a while. I kept thinking about my day yesterday, and how your life can change in twelve hours. Honestly, I don't expect much good from today either." Lloyd's face was perfectly illuminated to reveal the worry that had become permanently etched in his expression.

"Scott, why do bad things happen to good people?"

"That's a good question, but I think this might be a better question: Why do we allow things that happen, especially bad things, affect us more profoundly than the good? We humans take all of this bad in like a sponge filtering for food, but a sponge lets go after it gets what it needs."

"That's a bit simplistic, don't you think? I mean we are not in an ocean swimming around like a fish without feeling. We are people with emotions. Hurt and anger are emotions that are difficult to get past."

"This may be simple, but it's true, Lloyd. Let's see if I can get the idea out in its complete translation."

"I'm listening."

"Simplistically does a sponge change its attitude based on how difficult it is to filter food? The answer is no. It just continues doing its best. Humans, on the other hand, allow our environment to change us by controlling our attitude. Most humans walk around every day with a non-polar attitude."

"Non-polar attitude? What are you talking about?"

"It's being uncommitted to a particular view or philosophy to live by. Something everyone should do is commit to some form of philosophy in their daily lives. I would encourage you to choose a positive philosophy of approaching life with optimism. I know right now you find yourself in this pit, but think about the power you can have over your life by having a forgiving heart and adopting a positive attitude.

"Scott, that is a difficult thing for sure, and in some ways...," Lloyd trailed away for a moment. "I can't believe you are asking me to do that."

"I know but it truly is worthy of doing. I promise you that. I'm not just trying to sell this concept to you." Scott stared intently at Lloyd whose brow lowered toward his eyes. "I am living proof it can be done. I faced my own travesty in life. I carried the pain and burden of that event with me for years. I'm trying to help you circumvent a loop of existence not worth living through. Really this all comes down to will and the finer point of habits. I had to implement the habit of being positive to overcome the negative thoughts that came every day. Starting today, try to implement thoughts of confidence and optimism."

Lloyd, weary with the accusations and exhausted from the night, replied, "How do I do that? The entire world is crashing down on me."

"Lloyd, I have done a lot of living and a lot of learning. I read a book a few times by a guy named Charles Swindoll. In it he writes, 'Life is 10% what happens to us and 90% how we react to it.' This 10% going on with you admittedly is rough. What would be the problem with reacting with the outlook that God has a purpose for your life? Right now you are only seeing things from one perspective-- the perspective that everything is happening to you. What if you find God working in this event to create a turning point in the roadmap of your life in order to align you with His plan for your life? It's up to you to accept it."

"I want that, Scott. I really do, but it seems impossible at the moment."

"I have some ideas to help get you to a good place. They are more strategies than ideas, but it's all the same. Look, no one expects this to happen in a single moment or without help. I'm right here with you."

The exchange was interrupted as Lloyd's cell phone rang. "It's my wife."

"Okay, we can pick this up after your call."

"Hi, Liz."

"Lloyd, what is going on? I have had calls from several police departments around the area where you did that haul last week. Are they accusing you of something?"

"Yes, Liz, they are. They think I killed that missing guy." Lloyd's muscles tightened in his neck with stress. As they did, it exposed the blood vessels lying below the skin.

"I don't understand any of this. Ryan called here too. He said something about getting me your last paycheck since you wouldn't be around to get it."

"This is insane. This whole thing is insane. I can't believe that it got this far. The truth...funny how no one is looking for the truth; they are all just reacting." Clarity suddenly came over Lloyd. He realized what Scott was saying about the 10%, and how it was controlling him, his world, and the way this chapter of his life was being written.

"What happened, Lloyd? I can hear so much anxiety in your voice."

"I guess I am going to have to tell you." Lloyd drew in a deep breath and began telling her everything that had happened.

"Lloyd, I know you didn't and don't have anything to do with this missing man nonsense. I will pray for you and us. This will all be okay, I promise. I love you."

Lloyd stopped thinking about everything outside of this phone call as his mind drew a narrow focus on his wife's words. "Do you pray a lot?"

"Yes."

"Really?" Lloyd tried to hide the surprise in his voice, but his volume gave him away.

"Why does that surprise you so much?" Liz asked. "I started going to church when you are gone. I was going to ask you to come with me this weekend, but the last time I mentioned church to you, you made a face." Silence became the loudest noise in the call as the couple tried to figure out the course of a conversation that they both knew should have been face-to-face. "I bet you just made a face again," said Liz breaking the silence.

"Do you want me to say that I've changed my mind? Look at what I'm facing out here."

"Lloyd, I love you. I have always loved you and will always love you. I'm right beside you. Remember for better or worse? I will pray that something good comes from this."

"Okay, you pray. I will wait. I love you too, but I have to go." Lloyd ended the call by pressing the red button illuminated on the screen. "Well, that didn't go the way I thought it would. She was way calmer than I expected. I guess she has started praying. I didn't know that about her."

"This would be a good time to mention the strategies for getting and keeping a positive attitude. Reaction, as I mentioned, is one way to control our attitude, but that is really a byproduct of living it every day in deed. The first deed is gratitude."

"How is gratitude a deed? That's more of an emotion, isn't it?"

"Gratitude is giving or appreciating something or someone for a contribution they have made. So, going into a situation with the expectation that someone's contributing in some way to your benefit allows gratitude to naturally flow out. Take this recent thing with the police. Can you imagine the damage Ryan could do to your life by not getting the police involved? Eventually, this detective that burdens you now will be your key to freedom from this current derailment. The police are on your side, Lloyd, because you are innocent, and when that comes through in detailed clarity, you will have power over them in many aspects. The other step requires a bit of commitment on your part because this is a daily step. Every day read positive, motivational material and meditate about it."

"Daily seems like a lot. I don't even know where to find that much material. It seems like once a week would be more of an acceptable amount to commit to."

"I read this quote from Zig Ziglar: 'People often say that motivation doesn't last. Well, neither does bathing - that's why we recommend it daily.' Lloyd, this is the age of the Internet. We can find enough material to keep you bathed in motivation for a whole day all year long."

Both men found humor in Scott's statement giving an out loud laugh that Lloyd needed badly. "Thanks for calling me on that. I needed a laugh."

"I'm so glad you were able to find some humor in it too. The next suggestion for living a positive attitude is to journal daily." Glancing in Lloyd's direction, he caught the figure of his face. "I know by the look on your face that this isn't something that you likely want to do, but this can have immense pay off in your life. Journaling can open your mind to things you didn't really consider, and it can get things off your mind that you have considered for too long."

"You're right, Scott. It will take some work to get accustomed to doing that. I think that an advantage to keeping up with it would be to keep a record of at least where my mind is in that moment."

"Yes, that is very true. I like to compare it to hiking with a compass. I bet if this guy that is missing had a compass his chances of getting out of his predicament might have been a little better."

"Yes, without a doubt."

"The last strategic point might be the simplest, but it is just as important as all the others." Scott drew in his breath. Almost every time he had a willing listener, they would recoil from this and begin making excuses. Scott prepared his mind for objections. "The last strategy is exercise."

Lloyd chuckled a little and said, "What...what do you mean exercise? I drive a truck for a living, in case you forgot. How am I supposed to do that and exercise all day long?"

"No one said all day. We're talking two to two and one-half hours per week. I know everyone can do that. I used to watch that much worthless TV. After I started exercising, I realized I was wasting precious time thinking about why one fake character was trying to get another character who didn't exist in reality. I replaced the TV with exercise and added years and energy to my life."

"Okay, Scott, you got me on that. I do spend a considerable amount of time watching useless things. I could find time to do some exercise, I guess."

"Tell you what, Lloyd, I will go a step further. I will share some truck driver workout videos with you. I know how impressed you are going to be when you see how easy it is to work these into your schedule."

Their conversation concluded abruptly as the cell phone rang again. This time the caller ID read State Troop E. It was the detective. "Hello, this is Lloyd." He swallowed hard partly trying to ingest the anger spilling forth in his mind and partly keeping what little he had in his stomach where it belonged. His anxiety was reaching a crescendo.

"Sir, this is Detective Bernstein. I am calling to ask you to come to the station again as soon as possible. We can send a trooper out to bring you in if transportation is an issue this morning."

"Hello, Detective. Can you give me a moment to see if I can arrange for a ride? I really want to avoid the backseat of one of your patrol vehicles if I can." Covering the phone, Lloyd asked Scott, "Would you be able to give me a ride? They want me back at the highway patrol station this morning?"

"Of course. I'm here with you the whole way, Lloyd."

Small Changes

"Thank you, Scott. I can't tell you how much it means to me that you spent this time with me." Lloyd exited the cab of the semi and made his way to the entrance of the state patrol building. "I'm here to see Detective Bernstein," Lloyd stated in a near robotic voice talking to the speaker while pushing the black button to the side of the large, bulletproof glass.

The officer guarding that window replied quickly and coldly, "First and last name." Upon the pronouncement of his first and last name, the electromagnetic hold of the lock discharged.

Detective Bernstein emerged from the doorway into the lobby. "Thank you for coming in so quickly. If you could follow me, Sir, we can get started." He led Lloyd to a front room with a door.

"Not the interrogation room this time, Detective?"

The detective turned on the lights in the room motioning to the chair as he did. Lloyd followed the motion and sat down. "Sir," started Detective Bernstein.

"Please call me Lloyd, Detective."

"Alright, Sir...Lloyd." The detective took a pause as he looked at Lloyd a little stunned. He recalled the night before and the way Lloyd became so angry. It was almost like talking to a different person.

Lloyd took notice of the detective's stare and explained, "I'm not going to ask for forgiveness for last night. I feel that my outburst was in line with the anxiety I have felt since you and your officers put me face-first into an oily spot on the concrete. I will say, regardless of what news you may or may not have for me, that I am choosing to have a great attitude. I choose to be happy today and every day forward in spite of anything bad that comes along. I choose to be positive. So, Detective, how may I help you today?"

"I...uh...well...I'm sorry, Lloyd, that just took me by surprise. I have never had anyone set me straight like that before," said Detective Bernstein.

"I am really not trying to set you straight, Detective. We all have a choice: I can let these circumstances define me, or I can define myself as I go through them. The major difference, that I now understand, is that I have a choice, and it is up to me to either be weathered and worn or be the optimist with an outwardly positive attitude no matter the circumstances."

"That is a remarkable but difficult thing to do, in my opinion, especially when you are facing this incident that is currently taking place. You have given me something to think about. I will pray that I too can adopt an attitude of constant positivity." Once again someone in the conversation was speechless with surprise. Lloyd stared at the detective in bewilderment. "What is it, Lloyd?"

"Did you say pray? Here...at your job...to a suspect?"

"Yes, I did. I am a man of faith. As far as the job goes, I have broken no law or regulation by referring to prayer."

Lloyd, inching a smirk across his face, asked with cat-like curiosity, "What about the separation of church and state?"

The room became so silent that the humming of the air conditioner and the buzzing of the lights were very noticeable. The detective retrieved a remote control from his pocket, aimed it toward the ceiling, and pressed a button. "This doesn't pertain to the investigation in the least, so

I stopped the camera for a moment. Faith in my work is not a violation of anything. I express it often. I allow it to guide me through my everyday life on and off the job. As far as the separation of church and state goes, it's not in the constitution or any other official document. I would go as far as to say that anyone forcing me to hide my faith is in direct violation of my rights. They are the ones breaking the law. I know all the stuff they say about it, but the fact is the law is what it is. Now I'm turning the recording back on." The detective aimed the remote and pushed the button to continue the recording. "Are there any other details that you would like to give me about your accident?"

"I have given all the facts about this that I can. It is exactly the way I stated."

The door burst open as the detective's mouth formed the next word. The detective turned his attention toward the interrupter. "I'm in the middle of an interview; what's going on?"

"Sir, I think you should come with me. It pertains to the case and that dispatch we had earlier."

"Excuse me. I will be right back," said Detective Bernstein as he left the room. When he returned, the look on his face was different. Sitting down and slowly rubbing his hand on his tie, he took a moment to compose his thoughts before he spoke. "Sir, Lloyd, it appears you are free and clear of any and all charges pending against you. We received a call this morning from a park ranger that located parts of a body he found in a very closed off part of the park. They identified him as the missing man. They say an animal attacked him initially. The lacerations appear to be mountain lion marks. The rest of the damage is from scavengers like coyotes. I can take you to your truck at the impound lot and help you on your way if you like?"

"I would like that very much."

As the detective drove to the impound lot, he allowed his softer side to show. "Lloyd, I'm sorry this happened to you. I really hope you can forgive our department for being required to follow through on the anonymous tip we received. Everything fit together too conveniently. In our line of work, it's rare that things turn out the way they have. I guess I'm a little jaded by that."

"Detective, a good friend of mine has recently really helped me with my path in life. Not only is my new attitude based on being positive, but it's also built upward with gratitude. In retrospect I am grateful it was you and your department. Who knows how this would have turned out if instead of you a rookie detective who was only concerned about getting a conviction or forcing some sort of false confession had been assigned to this investigation. Because of all of this, I am learning what it means to have a forgiving spirit, and I can tell you, I have a lot of work ahead of me. I have done some work already. I have forgiven us both for the part that we shared in this."

"Thanks. Your truck is over there beyond the car impound." The car came to a halt at the guard shack where the detective showcased his badge to the officer standing guard over the lifeless metal behind the fence. As the guard signaled them on, the detective drove until they reached the truck impound area.

Lloyd opened the door of the car and turned to the detective. "Thanks for the ride and what you said earlier. I've never considered faith much before. It looks like maybe it's time I start. Hey, do you think a higher power might be trying to get my attention?"

"I don't see why not. I believe we all have a purpose, and God's will works in that purpose if we allow it. I know it's hard to accept that will. It's even more difficult to park your own will so that His can become greater."

Lloyd reached out his hand, and the detective reached back shaking Lloyd's hand. After saying goodbye, Lloyd turned and walked to his truck. Lloyd climbed into the cab, turned the key, and checked the gauges. After confirming everything was one hundred percent, he engaged the ignition by turning the key and brought the engine to life. Lloyd passed through the gate and headed toward the interstate. The feeling of freedom regained his mind as the ramp gave way to miles and miles stretched before and behind him. His thoughts were continually returning to Scott's words as he watched the white lines disappear. The exit to home and to Liz finally came into view. A sense of relief came over him. A sense of excitement that so much was behind him, yet so much lay ahead. Finally, he could rest easier.

Reflection

Liz was standing at the front door waiting for him. No words were necessary. The power of marriage is knowing what the partner needs the most without having to ask. She wrapped Lloyd in a very tight, warm, sheltering embrace. Tears of relief mixed with enthusiastic joy dropped on Lloyd's shoulder. From that same well of compassion, Liz asked, "Are you okay?"

"I'm okay, but we have a lot to talk about. I feel changed. I feel like I have become a different man not because of what happened to me but because of going through it."

"Tell me how you have changed."

"Well, to start I met this guy. He is like this oracle or something. He had these steps to living a more faithful life. We met at a restaurant and had lunch before the whole nightmare erupted. I called him after they arrested me. They came after me like I was a serial killer. It was the most traumatic thing I have ever been involved in. Anyway, Scott is his name, and I called him. He turned his truck around and came back for me."

"Let's sit down and talk some more. My legs are tired from pacing the living room and kitchen waiting for you to get here."

Lloyd continued, "So Scott came to the highway patrol station to pick me up after they released me. We talked about life until it got late and then again in the morning. We really spoke about living. You know, Liz, he said some things to me that have really stuck in my head."

"What did he say?"

"Well, the short of it is your life, my life, everyone's life is a message. It's something so profound and precious that we must take personal responsibility in the present. You take responsibility by becoming a person of action, helping others, giving care to others, and choosing your attitude."

"Choose your attitude? What does that mean?"

"It means controlling your reaction to everything life throws at you."

"Hmm," Liz cleared her throat in nervous anticipation. "Lloyd, may I say something to you and ask you to just listen until I'm finished?"

"I can do that," said Lloyd looking at Liz with a deep curiosity stretched over his face.

"I am really relieved to hear and see you so calm about this. I expected a different person to walk through the door tonight. I was prepared to hear your fluent, skilled use of profanity. I was so sure of it that I got the kids out of the house for the evening. Yet here in front of me is this collected man without even the hint of a curse word perched upon his lips. I think Scott has been a good influence on you. Here is the thing Lloyd: This past Sunday I went to church." Liz looked over at Lloyd gauging his receptiveness of the words she had just spoken. She watched her husband stare back with intrigue. She continued, "I know your feelings about church and religion. I listen to you say you don't see any point in going."

Lloyd interrupted, "Liz, it's okay, go on."

"Oh," she felt a smile creep across her face which she did her best to hide not wanting to presume his opinion had completely changed. "I was at church and the sermon was about how Jesus knew what he wanted in his life. He knew where it was going. He knew the path that he had to follow until the final day when he met his goal. The preacher went on to say that Jesus was a wise leader who knew he had to lead himself first before he could lead others. Did you know that Jesus wandered off into the wilderness too? Right after being baptized. I really wanted to tell you that on the phone the other night, but I didn't think you would have been as willing to listen as you have been so far. Jesus wandered into that desert alone until the devil showed up trying to wreck everything. He made every attempt to distract Jesus from his goal. Jesus guided himself through that horrid event and went on to gather his disciples. Then the preacher said the funniest thing...let me see...ah, yes, I think I have it: If Jesus would have driven a car, he would have been full speed with a full tank of goals. He would have burnt his headlights brightly because when your headlights are on, you know where you are going. He might have dimmed them to run the devil down. I thought that was pretty humorous, but I also thought the point that the preacher made was extraordinarily similar to the case you were facing. Lloyd, I have two simple questions for you: Do you know where you want your life to go from here? Have you chosen a path to follow daily?"

"Liz, it's really ironic that you bring that up. Scott was telling me things along that same line. He even has an emblem painted on his truck and trailer that says 'My Life is a Message.'"

"I know you aren't really a praying man, but I am going to make a suggestion that you pray and thank God for bringing Scott into your life, and maybe ask God what He has for you to fulfill. Maybe even ask what it is you should set out to accomplish. I hope for your sake that you're able to follow it when God answers you back."

"Will you?" Lloyd looked at the floor and then at the table studying the lines of the wood grain as he tried to summon the strength to do what is unnatural for a man to do-- ask for help. "Will you...do you think you could...," began Lloyd as he felt his composure of staying positive begin to shrink.

"Could I what?" Liz asked quietly in order to soften the edges for her husband.

"Could you help me pray later when we go to bed?"

Liz couldn't speak for a few seconds. She was thinking to herself that maybe the highway patrol had switched bodies with her real husband. "Yes! Of course! What are your goals for the future?"

"That's a good question." Lloyd looked off into the distance, staring at the clock on the stove that became a window into the future. His eyes glazed as he imagined what was possible for his life.

"A speaker who visited our church this week made a pretty insightful comment. He also talked about Jesus' leadership. He pointed out that God wants us to have success in our spiritual life and our work. Then he said what I think was the most memorable part of all: 'Destinations to success require roadmaps created by you before starting the journey, and don't forget to use the rest stops along the way. Take that rest time to improve your health, spirituality, relationships, career, education, self, and family.'

"His story was really powerful to me. He started off with his background. He grew up in an orphanage. When he got old enough to really reason, he became angry mostly with the thoughts and feelings of being abandoned. Then he acted on that anger. He was sent to juvenile jail several times. After the anger subsided, he became really depressed. He compared it to being in a dark, smoke-filled hallway where you can't catch your breath. You are always fighting for clean air. Everyone can see you, but no one can really reach you. The sadness just couldn't be shaken.

"One day a friend of his named Dwayne and he were talking in gym class. Dwayne asked if he believed in God. He said he didn't really know. He asked Dwayne if God abandons people as his parents did. Dwayne told him you really have to get to know this kind of a father who is always there for you. Then Dwayne asked him to go with him and his family to church on Sunday. He said after church he drilled that preacher for thirty-five minutes. He took those answers with him that day and carried them with him for a long while. After contemplating the answers he was given, he went back to that church to be baptized. Eventually, with God's help, the smoke in his life cleared.

"He became a very successful entrepreneur. He instilled a culture of faith in his company and made the point that without a defining culture for people to cling to, everyone kind of floats around with their own idea of what to strive for. According to him, culture is the biggest key element in business and life since it affects everything. He said his employees were always his first priority. He didn't force his faith on his unbelieving employees, but he did expect them to observe the company philosophy or mission which was clearly posted in the handbook.

"I did a little research after I got home, and sure enough, that company was listed in the <u>Forbes</u> '200 Best Places to Work For' ten years in a row. I believe it's still listed too. He travels around the country now doing work for charities. It was a truly fascinating talk."

"You must have really paid attention to remember all of that. He must have been intriguing."

"He was. Let's see..." Liz got up from her seat and rustled through some papers that were on the kitchen counter. "Here it is. The flyer they handed out with the gentleman's information."

Handing the folded paper to Lloyd, he examined it casually, and then something very familiar caught his eye. Looking up slowly in disbelief, he turned to Liz. "Do you think all of this is happening for a purpose?"

Looking directly into his eyes and studying her husband's face, she thought for a moment whether to give the answer he would accept or the answer she knew was the truth. "Yes, I do. The truth is that God has a purpose for us all, but everyone's purpose may be different. It's up to us to seek that purpose out."

"You know, Scott said about the same thing. Do you think that this Scott, the multimillionaire; the business owner; and the minister charity worker from the Three Cross Ministry, could be the same person? Do you think maybe my purpose is being forcibly shown to me?"

"I don't think that God would force his way into your life. After all, if you don't have ears to hear it or eyes to see it, then what good would it be to show it to you? I think you must have been doing a lot of contemplating about your life lately."

"Well, sure I have. I mean our financial situation is always weighing on me. We wanted the land and the house, but everything has gone up. I feel really trapped by it a lot of times. I just can't bring myself to the idea of selling and forcing the kids to move to a different school. I blame myself since I was the driving force to buy it. Sometimes I find myself talking out loud for help."

"You really need to learn to let things go and forgive yourself."

"It's really hard to forgive. I have never really known how to do it. Scott suggested I forgive Ryan, and now you want me to forgive myself. How? How do I do that?"

"You simply just ask and receive."

"Can it really be that easy?"

"No, it's not easy. Sometimes simple is hard. It comes down to the life you want to live. It's a decision that you make every day you open your eyes and every night when you close them. It's the breathing of your soul. You take in the things that happen to you like inhaling. Then it's a choice to exhale. Exhaling means life, but keeping that air inside your lungs ultimately means death. The spirit is the same way. If you keep all of these offenses to yourself, eventually your spirit won't grow, and if you aren't growing, you're dying. Breathing is a strength, not a weakness. Likewise, forgiveness is a strength, not a weakness."

"Do you really believe that?" said Lloyd. His childlike curiosity in the sincerity of his question began showing through his doubt.

Liz's face was serious and determined to make an impact on her husband. She wanted to help create change in him for a better tomorrow. "Yes, Lloyd, I do," she said in a gravity weighted tone.

The ringing of the phone broke the conversation. Lloyd rose to answer it.

Terminated

"Hello."

"Hello, Lloyd?"

"Yes, this is Lloyd."

"Hi, this is Sarah Freeman."

"Hi, Sarah, how is Human Resources lately?"

"Well, to be honest, today is a bit puzzling. I'm calling to let you know we are going to need your remote door key, your badge, and your tablet returned to us within the next few days."

"I'm sorry, but what are you talking about?"

"Didn't Ryan explain to you when you got in?"

"Explain what exactly?"

"Hold for just a moment." The phone speaker turned jukebox while Lloyd waited. He could feel sweat of angered anticipation on his neck, brow, and back. Everywhere stress could leak its way into his existence, it did. The music became painful in his ear. His new mindset was being tested.

"Hello, Lloyd, this isn't the way this is usually handled. I have to inform you, unfortunately over the phone, that we received notice of your termination from your supervisor."

"My supervisor? What was the reason for termination?" Lloyd said staring at Liz as he said the words. She put her coffee cup on the table and listened intently to the conversation regarding the future of their family.

"The most I can tell you is that it sites insubordination. Other than that, I'm not really at liberty to discuss this any further over the phone. I have been instructed to ask you to return all company property within a few days in order to receive your last paycheck."

"Do you know what this is going to do to me? To my family? My supervisor is the cause of all of this. He is irrational and unprofessional. Have you even looked into this?"

"Currently, I'm not at liberty to discuss those details any further."

"Who can discuss them further?"

"I will have to refer this to Bill, the vice-president of HR. I really can't do any more than that, Lloyd. I'm really sorry."

As the phone call ended, he let out a sigh of exaggerated anger. His heart racing against his mind's thoughts, Lloyd found himself on the edge of good versus evil, a place where his life could alter very quickly. His thoughts were irrational. He stormed down the hallway with Liz chasing after him.

"Lloyd, what is it? What are you going to do?"

"It's best you don't know what's coming!"

"Lloyd!" Liz yelled as sobs of crying began to surface with her pleas.

"They can only push me so far. I'm taking care of my biggest problem today...RIGHT NOW!" Retrieving a small firearm from his gun safe, Lloyd's hands were shaking with anger.

"What are you doing? This isn't you! You have to stop! What about what you said earlier?"

Lloyd stormed passed her and out to his truck. Opening the truck door, jumping into the driver's seat, and closing the door was all one motion. As soon as the truck started, he could see Liz running up to the side screaming for him to wait. Before she could reach the truck door, he slammed the truck into drive, stepped hard on the accelerator, and sent gravel flying into the air and yard as the tires broke traction. Lloyd looked in the rearview mirror and caught his own glaring gaze staring back. Wanting to avoid his own reflection, he looked ahead.

Purpose

Dust was clouding the air in the quickly approaching distance. As his eyes focused, another vehicle appeared in his frame of vision. The sun reflected off the chrome of the approaching bumper and sent light dancing through the window breaking Lloyd's concentration about how furious he was. In that blinking moment, Lloyd realized the gap between him and the other vehicle was closing extremely fast. The point of no return for a collision was approaching. Lloyd locked the brakes. Sliding back and forth in tail-wagging fashion, the truck began grinding to a halt and came to a sudden stop. Lloyd moved the gear to P and rolled down his window to talk to the occupant of the nearby parked vehicle.

The other truck had come to a less dramatic stop opposite Lloyd. A thick cloud of dust from the two vehicles floated in the air. To Lloyd's utter astonishment, out stepped a person that he least expected to see on this road at this very difficult time. Lloyd leaned forward to peer through his windshield. His emotions overtook him. Lloyd choked back his expressions the best he could, but deep within him stirred the question and out of his mouth came the words, "I see you working in my life now, God." Lloyd admitted to himself that this was not just a coincidence. A familiar figure was walking towards him.

"Lloyd, are you okay?"

"I'm okay. I...I..."

"What is that in the seat next to you?"

Tears began flowing down Lloyd's face. Scott flung the truck door open and hugged Lloyd tightly in a protective embrace. Scott began praying out loud begging God to show mercy to this man. As Lloyd regained control over his breathing, Scott loosened his embrace.

"That's the only solution I could see. There just wasn't anything else I could think to do," Lloyd said with his head shamefully pointed toward the floorboard. "I'm so sorry. I just couldn't stay positive. Now my career is gone. I don't know what I'm going to do. What are you doing out here? How did you find me?"

"You keep forgetting this is the age of the Internet."

"Oh," Lloyd said sinking back into his own thoughts.

"What do you say we go back to your house and talk this out?"

"There is nothing to talk about, Scott. I'm done. I'm ruined. We are going to lose the land and the house. All my struggles will have been in vain."

"You look at me. Do you really think this is it? Do you really think doing whatever you were going to do with that in the seat next to you is the answer to anything? How would anything have gotten better with that?"

"He deserves what he was going to get."

"He deserves something else, and that isn't it. Things will change, and doing something like that will just cause you to miss out on all the good in store for you. Why don't you hand me the gun?"

Scott stuck his hand out and was met with a cold angry stare.

"I'm not sure I'm done with it yet."

"Fine, have it your way." Shocked with Scott's comment, Lloyd watched his friend walk away. Scott returned to his truck and moved it out of the way giving enough room for Lloyd's truck to pass by. Scott opened his door, stepped out, shut the door, and locked it as if he was planning to leave the truck parked. Lloyd watched all of this with a deep curiosity about what Scott was planning. Scott walked to the passenger side of Lloyd's truck. Thinking that Scott was trying to take the gun from him, Lloyd quickly grabbed it. Scott opened the door and sat down in Lloyd's truck. "All right, Lloyd, if you are going to go do this, then let's go. I'm going with you."

"I'm not getting you involved in anything like that, Scott."

"C'mon, let's go. You've got murder on your mind. Let's just go get it over with." Lloyd stared at Scott searching his face for a clue telling if he was joking or serious. "I'm serious. Let's get going." Scott turned to Lloyd and nodded his head towards the road in a motion that said this way.

"I will not allow you in this mess, Scott."

"Then give me the gun, and let's go back to your house."

Lloyd took a deep breath as he considered Scott's advice. Reaching behind his back, he pulled the gun from the crack between the two seats. "Here."

"Thank you, Lloyd."

"I don't think I can look Liz in the eye right now. Honestly, I'm ashamed of my actions."

"I don't know what happened at home, but it sounds like she was probably against this idea. Am I right?"

"Yes, she was screaming at me to stop. She was so scared."

"You should go home. I can wait here for a bit while you talk to her."

Feeling extremely frustrated, Lloyd yelled out as he beat his hands on the steering wheel. "Why is this happening? Why me? I'm not a horrible person. I don't do terrible things. This should not be happening to me."

A slight laugh emerged from Scott. "I'm sorry. I like to look at things from the perspective of learning. Where is the lesson? How does this fit into the path that God has for me?"

"I've certainly learned a lot from this ordeal. I have learned you can never let your guard down. You can never wash your truck after you hit a deer without first consulting the FBI, highway patrol, and the CIA. I have learned that the harder I try, the further back I seem to go."

"Come on, Lloyd. Seriously, that is your big take away from all of this?"

"No, not really, but it sure seems like all that stuff is true."

"Do you still have that napkin I drew the picture on for you at the restaurant?"

"Yes." Lloyd fished for his wallet. "Here it is," he said as he took it out of its leather surroundings and unfolded it carefully.

"What does that say in the middle?"

"It says purpose."

"What is your purpose?"

"I won't lie to you. Right now I don't feel like I have much of a purpose."

"Oh, my friend, you have much more purpose than you think. You are going to get back up and climb out of this predicament that you are in. Your purpose right now is to find that decided heart and forgive others who have wronged you. I'm certain that is the path that leads to the greatest outcome for all of us."

"Are you saying that a decided heart is going to suddenly make things different?"

"I'm saying that a j-o-b doesn't define you. Your career may or may not be over. If you find yourself deciding which things make you the happiest and excite you the most, what can stop you? I personally believe you are in this test of a lifetime to show your determination and what you can get from life. I personally believe God is going to use this incident to make the best plan for your life. As I said before, it's up to you to walk in that plan. You may not agree with me, but I will tell you from my heart and all of my life experiences, that sometimes, well actually every time, it's times like this you uncover your unique ability. When you put a superior ability together with passion, it's an unstoppable force. I also personally believe that this unique ability can lead to great value for yourself and others."

"You know, I was thinking the other day about how much I like helping others."

"Hey, that's a great start."

After a long pause, Lloyd said, "I think it's time to go to the house."

"I think you're right, Lloyd. You shouldn't have ever been on this road in the first place with the intent you had in your mind. I will give you and Liz some time to talk." Scott opened the door of the truck and got out walking back to his own truck.

Lloyd turned the truck around and went back to his house where Liz was waiting in anxious concern.

Prayer

Watching from the front porch, Liz saw dust rising on the gravel road. She wiped her face dry with the sleeve of her t-shirt. She hoped that it was not her mom bringing the kids home. Her mood was still distraught and filled with worry for her husband. Lloyd came into view, and Liz drew in a breath of relief. Her husband had not done the very awful thing he seemed to be set on doing earlier. He was safely on his way back.

Lloyd drove slowly from the road to the driveway. Seeing the ruts that his exploding anger had dug into the rocks caused him to feel even more shameful for his actions. He sat in the idling truck for a moment trying to find a way to break the ice with Liz. Reluctantly, he turned the key to the ignition killing the engine. Silence. Lloyd contemplated his next move. Where would he find the money to make the next house payment? Where would he find the money to do anything? The desperation came flooding back, but this time rather than becoming angry, he turned toward Heaven. "Most people think you are up, but I don't know where you are. I haven't talked to you in years. I don't blame you if you don't want to talk to me. Here I am at the lowest point I think I have ever been. If this is the path I am supposed to be on, could you please light the path a little? Could you show me a way to my unique gift? Could you help me a little? I'm pretty low at this point."

Liz was standing right by his door window as he opened his eyes. She backed away from the door so Lloyd could open it. As he did, Liz could see the exhaustion on his face. She could see the marks of the tears that he cried earlier. Her heart was heavy for her husband. "I'm so glad you came back. We can get through this, whatever it is, together."

"Liz, I'm so sorry I put you through all of this. I need to tell you about the phone call I got that set me off."

"Okay. Why don't we go in the house? It's hot out here."

"In a moment. I'm kind of waiting for something. Before we get interrupted, I want to tell you what happened. They fired me. I didn't even know that it had happened. Ryan put in my termination without even really telling me it was official. I mean he threatened me, but you know how he is.

He makes threats to everyone all the time about firing them. The culture of the company, if there is even a culture there or at least at this local branch, is intimidation. That's all that guy ever does is intimidate everyone with his position and their jobs."

"Is there anything we can do?"

"I don't know. I was going to set up a meeting with his supervisor when I got back, but I didn't have a chance."

Liz looked over her shoulder to gaze out at their property while quietly lamenting over the idea that all of it could be gone soon. She saw the dust rising once again on the gravel road. "Who is coming down our road?"

"That's what I have been waiting on. It's my friend Scott. He showed up out of nowhere. As I was driving out of here, he had just gotten off the main road and started down our road. We met nearly head-on since I was driving so fast. He is pretty much the reason I didn't follow through with that stupid idea I had. He waited for a while so you and I could talk privately first."

Scott's big white tractor with no trailer came into view and rolled over the crunching gravel. He drove closer and came to a stop. Rolling down the window, Scott said, "Where do you want me to park?" Moving the truck to where Lloyd motioned, Scott stopped the engine. He climbed out and walked towards Lloyd and Liz. As he made his way towards them, Liz began to recognize that this wasn't just Lloyd's friend but also the man who had spoken at her church. This was the multi-million dollar, entrepreneur orphan who had gone from angry to saved because a friend and his parents had taken the time to be a part of his life. This was the founder of the Three Cross Ministry. "Hi," Scott said as he approached them.

"Hey, Scott," Lloyd said. "This is my wife Elizabeth, but everyone calls her Liz. Liz, this is my new friend Scott who dropped in today to check on me after last week's incident." Scott reached out his hand to shake Liz's. After shaking hands, Liz suggested they go inside.

Faith

"You have a beautiful home."

"Thank you so much for that, Scott. Please come in and make yourself at home." The three sat in the living room. Lloyd was still not completely coherent from the events that had played out during the morning time. Liz broke the silence by reaching over to grab the paper she had received when she went to church the night the visitor came from the Three Cross Ministry. "So, Scott, hearing everything Lloyd has told me about you, I can't help but confirm you are the same person who visited our church very recently. I wasn't close enough to really see your face clearly."

"Oh my, yes, that was me. You were there?"

"I was. Lloyd and I both thought that it might be you, but what a coincidence that you, of all people, would be the one to hear him on his CB radio and respond."

"True enough, Liz, that does seem like a coincidence, but I think walking in God's plan every day led me to Lloyd."

Lloyd looked up from the floor. His eyes were bright, and his expression was such that something needed to escape his mind quickly before he lost the thought. "I'm done trying to do this on my own. I can't do it by myself. Scott, I want what you have. I want to be a person of faith. I need to get this all out right now. I don't want to get old and think back to what if. What if I had changed my direction in life back then? What if I had listened to all the things my friend Scott and my wife were always trying to tell me? I want to take each day and make it the best day possible. I don't want to keep trying alone either. I asked God earlier to help me and to light my path. I admitted that I haven't spoken to him in a while. I told him if you don't want to talk to me, I understand, but I really need help."

"Lloyd, the only way forward is not looking back. Start living your life looking forward not looking back. God can become the center of everything you do. This includes your business, your personal life, and your professional life. It's up to us to align ourselves in our faith. Let me share another strategy with you and that is preparation. Preparation for a good tomorrow is to live a great today. Start each day from here on out with a simple motto: I am a person of great faith. I believe all of my talents and gifts come from God. That motto will keep you centered on the source of all the goodness that is going to happen in your life."

"I like that. I'm going to write that down and stick it to my mirror so that I can see it every single day. This is going to be a culture shift and a new mindset."

Liz was overwhelmed with her husband's dramatic change of heart. Her eyes welled with tears. "Lloyd, I can't tell you how happy and relieved I am to hear you say these things."

"Lloyd, there is something to consider: Your forgiveness to Ryan for the deeds that he has done."

Lloyd looked back to the floor. "I'm sorry, Scott, but I just can't get that out yet. I really just can't."

"Hopefully, it will come to you at the right time."

"If I'm going to walk in God's plan intentionally, how do I start, Scott?"

"It all starts and continues with that middle line that I drew for you on that napkin in your wallet. It comes down to purpose. You do it on purpose. You do it to find your purpose. Then once you have found your purpose, you do it to fulfill your purpose. I used to be lost in this world with zero purpose. I wasn't looking for one, but after I accepted God as my guiding beacon in all things, my life changed. I went from leading the way to prison to leading my board room. I think it really comes down to wanting to be a person of great faith."

Liz turned to Lloyd. "I have waited for so long to hear you say these things and to feel these things. I hate saying this out loud, but I'm almost glad this has happened to you. This is a big turning point. I know things are going to be tough on both of us, but I have faith every day that God will provide a path. I am in this with you, Lloyd."

"And so am I," said Scott.

"I can't exactly sing songs about what has happened to me so far, but I am glad you two are behind me. What should we do next?"

"Lloyd, I think you need to seek resolution about this situation at your job. I think it will be hard for you to move on personally and professionally if you don't."

"I agree with Scott. I think you might need to talk with the HR people again at least to explain your side of things. If that doesn't get some closure for you, nothing really will."

"You are both right. I can't move forward living my best day if I have this thing tied to me like a leash dragging me back to the past."

"It's a step, Lloyd, and like Liz said, this very well might give you some closure. It's one step today, then another tomorrow. Before long you will be running again. Running towards a new goal. You said you like helping people, so let's see if we can get you to live your dream."

"I like that. Okay, so here I go." Lloyd rose from the couch and took some deep breaths. He could feel his heart racing with the thoughts of the conversation rebutting everything that he said. The fresh air in his lungs cleared his mind of the negative thoughts and replaced them with positive ideas of what his outcome should and would be. Lloyd had turned his positive thinking back on, and those thoughts felt great. This momentum pushed him towards the phone. He found himself a quiet spot to talk. He took out his cellular phone and opened it to an Internet browser. Typing "ceo of forward trucking," he located a website that listed the CEO Larry Hawthorn 555-555-5555. Lloyd dialed the number.

"Hello, Mr. Hawthorn's office. This is Cindy. How may I help you?"

"Hi, Cindy, my name is Lloyd. May I speak with Mr. Hawthorn?"

"May I have the reason for your call? Mr. Hawthorn is in a meeting at the moment."

"I can wait. How long do you think he will be?"

"Oh no, Sir, I wouldn't want you to do that. It might be a while."

On the other end of the line, Mr. Hawthorn's voice could be heard as he opened the door talking to none other than Bill, the vice-president of Human Resources. "Bill, I appreciate you telling me all of this and helping me get out in front of a potential bombshell to our company. If our partners ever heard that we had this kind of trouble internally, we might not keep them very long."

"It's the least I could do, Mr. Hawthorn. I believe the decision we came too is the appropriate and right thing to do. I know this probably isn't the exact moment I should mention this, but I came across a book that I bought from Amazon the other day. It was called *Positive Culture Wins In Business and Life*. This book really got me thinking that we should develop a culture for our company. This book tells how to do that. I think it would be an addition to the bottom line of our corporate profits, but more importantly, a profit to our employees."

"Let's discuss that in more detail soon. I like where you are headed with that, and if we can avoid something like we are facing now, that would be excellent."

"Agreed, Mr. Hawthorn. I will put something together to present to you next week."

"Bill, that sounds great."

Suddenly Cindy realized that Lloyd might be able to hear the background chatter and swiftly announced, "Please hold," followed with slow jazz music. After a brief hold, she said, "Sir, are you still there?"

"Yes, I'm here."

ꞏ I am transferring you to Mr. Hawthorn now."

"Thank you."

"Good afternoon. This is Larry Hawthorn."

"Mr. Hawthorn, this is Lloyd. I need to discuss some things with you about your company and one of your supervisors."

"Yes, Lloyd, I'm sure you do. Would you like to do that over the phone, or should we meet face to face?"

"I don't mind doing it over the phone."

"That's fine with me too. Listen, before you get started, may I say something?"

"Of course, you can, Mr. Hawthorn."

"Thanks. After your termination was processed, one of our HR staff contacted Bill, our vice-president in HR. It's a company policy as much as it is a safeguard that we pull the personnel file to find out if the termination was justified. When your file was pulled, we found that we had an exemplary employee without a blemish to speak of on record. Well, you don't get as old as I am and not learn some things. I know when there is trouble. We contacted your supervisor regarding the matter. Bill got on a plane and went to speak with him. The only thing he could give us as a reason was telling us to turn on the TV and watch the newscast about the search for a missing guy. Your supervisor alleged that you killed this guy with your truck. When Bill got back, we discussed the whole thing. We both concluded that you couldn't have had anything to do with this. The problem is that we got to this way too late in the process. We both heard that the charges were dropped as soon as they found that poor guy. Bill and I both agreed that it would be best to let Ryan go. We clearly don't need someone like that bringing down the morale the way he was in that office. We really do not need someone that harasses an employee of your stature by calling the police and giving a false report. We need more people like you, not less. Lloyd, I am going to make you an offer. You should consider this carefully because it could have a legal impact."

"I'm listening, Sir."

"I will get right to it then. We would like to offer you a settlement. If you have already spoken to a lawyer, you will want to discuss or have our legal expert speak with your lawyer about it before making any decisions."

"I would like to hear the offer myself first, if you don't mind?"

"Very well then, Lloyd. We would like to offer you $250,000 to make restitution for the damages you incurred through this. I'm an honest man, and I will tell you if you go to a lawyer and pursue a case, you might end up with more. I think it's a fair deal though, and we could bypass the lawyer taking a cut. We would also like to offer you another job. Not driving, but this time in the office. Lloyd, the offer we are making regarding the money does not disappear if you accept the job or not. It's entirely up to you."

Lloyd couldn't believe this was happening. His heart began to pound. He started feeling gratitude. He was grateful that the CEO of the company he worked for actually valued him. The feeling of being appreciated overtook him for a moment. Had Scott and Liz been right this whole time? The lump that had formed in Lloyd's throat made it impossible for him to speak at the moment.

Mr. Hawthorn continued, "Lloyd, I'm sure this a big decision legally speaking, and I understand your silence. Please consider it."

Lloyd finally regained his composure. "Yes, I will do that, Mr. Hawthorn. When would you like an answer?"

"Well, we have the opening now in regard to the job, so the sooner the better. Discuss it with your lawyer and your wife, if you would like. Let me know when you have made a decision."

"I can do that, Mr. Hawthorn. Is there a better number to call, or should I continue using this one?" Mr. Hawthorn and Lloyd exchanged phone numbers.

Lloyd made his way to the living room where Scott and Liz waited patiently and nervously. "You are not going to believe what just happened," Lloyd announced as he walked to the couch and sat down. "I can't believe that just a few hours ago I was set to make the biggest mistake of my life. I just received the largest reversal I can ever remember." Lloyd relayed the conversation nearly word for word to Scott and Liz.

"Lloyd, I feel like I can really open up to you about this now. You know earlier today you said you wanted to be a person of great faith. I'm going to level with you. One of the hardest things to do is to surrender your own power. I don't mean your own will. You keep that. Surrender your own power to the idea that your successes and failures really come from you. They don't. From a faith standpoint and from here on out, acknowledging God leading you through life is the lantern for your path. If you listen for his voice, you will hear it. That voice will help you find the talents and gifts you possess. That voice will also tell you how best to use them. It's going to be important to remind yourself daily that God gives us all that we have and all that we have to offer."

"I will do that to the best of my ability, Scott. Hey, Liz, I was thinking that I would like to go to church with you on Sunday. Would that be okay? I think I need to check it out.

Scott, could you stay until then? I would really like for you to be there too. I would be so excited for you to go with us."

"I will make a couple of arrangements and stay here. I told you I would be here for you all the way, and this is a big step."

"Now what do you think I should do about the offer?"

"Good question," said Liz. The three sat and discussed everything in detail until late into the night. They reached a mutual decision about Lloyd's future.

Reconciled

That Sunday they all went to church. Lloyd seemed nervous. Liz noticed that he was fidgeting with everything. "Lloyd, is everything alright with you this morning? You don't have to be nervous about going to church. No one is going to bite you."

"I'm not nervous about going to church. It's what I want to do."

Liz was standing in the light of their bathroom. Her face reflected in the mirror as he messed with his hair. He loved the way her eyes looked in this light. Her eyes always seemed to calm him down, at least nearly always. "What do you want to do at church?"

"Well, I was watching a religious channel the other night after everyone went to bed. They had some people that would get up and tell their story or…"

"Testimony?"

"Yeah, that's what they called it. Testimony. Anyway, they were standing up and confessing how they used to be in their lives. Some of those stories were pretty awful. One was about a lady that was hooked on drugs and used prostitution to make money. She said that she heard God speaking to her one night. You know kind of like Scott said about listening for the voice? Anyway, she was rescued from that life. I started contemplating that there are other people that need to hear my story. Maybe as I am changing my life by taking the steps I am taking, I can inspire others."

"That's a good point. Do you think you can do it? Get up in front of all those people?"

"How many people are we talking about? I mean it's a church. A hundred or so?"

Liz chuckled and said, "I think it's a little more than that." Liz walked to the nightstand where she kept her Bible and pulled out the handout the church gives to each attendee. She opened the page pointing to the attendance from the week before.

"Seven hundred twenty-three," Lloyd read aloud. "Is this a big church?"

"I would say bigger than average."

Lloyd shrugged his shoulder as he settled on the idea. "Seven or seven hundred I feel like I should tell my story. I have a decided heart about this, and I want to help people by sharing my experience." Liz agreed, but Lloyd withheld the idea from Scott. Not for any reason other than he was preoccupied with trying to formulate an outline in his mind of exactly what he would say.

As they arrived at the church, they were greeted at the door. Liz pointed a man out to Lloyd. "That's who you need to talk to so you can complete your goal today," she whispered in Lloyd's ear. Liz introduced her husband and Scott who was recognized by many from his last visit. Lloyd broke away to talk to the man Liz had pointed out. When he returned to Liz's side, they walked into the sanctuary. After being seated, once again Liz leaned over and whispered to Lloyd, "Did he agree to let you speak?"

"He said it was unusual for a first-timer to want to do that, and that he would be happy to hear what I had to say."

Church was underway. The singing was finished, announcements about an upcoming potluck were made, and the time had come for the testimony. "We have someone today that has a story to share with everyone. He is a first-time visitor. He told me a little about what he wants to share. I think everyone will be interested in what Lloyd has to say. Lloyd, come on up."

Lloyd made his way to the front of the church. Taking the mic into his hand, he held it up to his lips and began speaking. "Hello, my name is Lloyd. Just a couple of weeks ago, I was on the outside of God's plan, but something happened to me that has changed my life forever. I hope to help change someone else's life too."

Scott, sitting in the audience, listened as Lloyd told his story from beginning to end. Astonished with his ability to hold the audience's attention as he went through each event and the eloquence of his speaking, Scott began to get an idea. Scott heard that voice he told Lloyd about just a few days prior. The voice that leads you on your path. Being disciplined Scott always tried to follow without hesitating. As Lloyd drew to a close, the entire sanctuary erupted with applause, and "Praise God" was shouted all over the place.

Lloyd shook the hand of the last person on the way out the church door and walked over to Scott. "Hey, Lloyd, could I buy you two lunch? I have an idea that needs to get out of my head and into the world. It's an exciting one that I hope you both will agree to."

Sitting in the restaurant once again with Scott, Lloyd said, "Kind of funny this all began in a restaurant, and here we are in a restaurant again with something new to talk about."

Scott gazed off in the distance thinking about their first encounter. He said, "I hadn't given that much thought, but you are right, it is rather ironic. While you were speaking today, I had a thought. What if you took the settlement and declined the position?"

Liz interjected "I thought we all came to a mutual decision about that. Lloyd was going to continue his career. Why would he quit now after everything that he has gone through?"

"That's exactly why because of everything you have gone through. You said that you like helping people, right? That it's one of your passions in life, right? Well, what if I said that I thought one of your unique gifts is telling people uplifting things?"

"You mean like motivational speaking?"

"Yes, exactly that."

"I never really ever considered anything as ambitious as that."

"This is," Liz said, "your turning point. You can't really go back to being the guy you were before all of this began."

"That's true. I have changed."

"You would be home more and get to do things with the family more often," said Liz.

"Here is what came to me. We set the company up with a little investment from the settlement, and I will kick in a big investment. We can keep it faith-based but reach a broader audience through our marketing. We could reach millions of people. What do you think?"

"I think it's going to be like starting a merry-go-round."

Liz looked at Lloyd as if he was crazy. "What do you mean?"

"Remember when we were kids, and we would get on the merry-go-round? One of us would have to push everyone else. The hardest part was that first step; the second was hard but not as difficult as the first. Once we got it going and everyone was cheering 'Faster, Faster,' you jumped on and watched the world in high-speed, circular motion. This is going to be a lot like that, I think. Scott, you remember saying the other night that I just have to get my momentum going?"

"Sure, I remember it was when we discussed the decision about your offer."

"I think this is right along with that line. Let's do it! What do you say, Liz? Are we in?"

Looking at both men with excitement in her eyes and a smile on her face, she agreed to move forward.

Monday soon came. Once again Lloyd was staring at the phone as he finished his second cup of coffee. He was hesitant about making the call to Mr. Hawthorn. Lloyd knew he had been led to this point in his life. He knew this was the right thing to do. As he thought more and more, and the minutes wore on, Lloyd made reconciliation with himself and his career. Strangely enough, at that moment he discovered that he was in the process of forgiving Ryan. After all, if he hadn't made that very bad decision, nothing would have ever changed. He would probably be on the road in a truck right now. The only thing holding him back was FEAR—False Evidence Appearing Real. Lloyd took out a pen and paper and wrote a note about that. He also took out his cell phone, opened the screen, and went to contacts. Today he was going to reconcile two things in his life: Begin a new career, and forgive Ryan out loud so that he couldn't take it back. He would never again own such hatred he thought. Scott was right. Forgiveness is the only path. With that final thought, Lloyd picked up the phone and dialed Mr. Hawthorn.

Moving Forward

"Hi, Mr. Hawthorn, it's Lloyd."

As he explained his decision, Mr. Hawthorn became interested in the idea as well. "Lloyd, I totally understand, and I appreciate you taking the settlement. We will have that to you as soon as legal signs off on it. I would, however, be interested in hearing more about this idea you and your friend have created."

"Very good, Sir, I will keep you in the loop as we go forward," Lloyd said. The two men said their goodbyes as the call concluded. As he pushed the button on the phone to disconnect, he realized he was disconnecting his career at the same time.

Lloyd yelled for Liz. "What is it, Lloyd?"

"Liz, Mr. Hawthorn wants to bring me in as a guest motivational speaker once we get everything developed. Our first semi-scheduled gig!"

"Wow, Lloyd, that is great! Have you told Scott yet?"

"No, not yet. There is one more call I need to make this morning. I will talk with Scott after I get done with this one."

"Who are you calling?"

"I'm calling Ryan."

"What on earth would you do that for? Why do you want to reopen that line of communication?"

"I have to do this. You both said that forgiveness is the best path. Today I am ready to forgive Ryan for what happened. I'm not saying we are going to be best friends or anything."

Laughing Liz said, "I would hope not. You are a better judge of character than that, I am sure." Liz turned and started walking back to the utility room. "I have to fold the rest of these clothes, and you need your privacy for this one. I will keep the kids occupied so that it's quiet."

"Thank you. Wish me luck."

"I will say a prayer for you," Liz said, her voice trailing away down the hall.

Lloyd returned to the kitchen where he seemed to do his best thinking lately. Acting more out of impulse than thought, he grabbed his cellular phone and called Ryan.

Faithful Living

The business became a reality. Lloyd, Scott, and Liz worked together as a team to develop the business and the material. After working tirelessly to get the speech, images, and inflection perfect, Lloyd contacted Mr. Hawthorn who graciously and enthusiastically kept his invitation open. Lloyd went to see his former employer for the first time as the leader he knew he was meant to be. He went to inspire his former coworkers with his story, purpose, and the greatest ten points ever developed.

Lloyd was asked to come back ten more times which both pleased and humbled him. The eleventh request; however, couldn't be honored. The speaking business had grown so much that Lloyd simply couldn't make it work on the eleventh year. The Team, as they had begun calling themselves, had set goals ten years prior, and in this eleventh year of business, those goals were coming into full focus. The business was very successful.

The Team agreed to ask Mr. Hawthorn for the opportunity to give the opening speech at the convention center. This seminar was a crowd of six thousand people, and all six thousand had come to hear Lloyd and several others speak and do workshops for three days. Today was Lloyd's turn to deliver his keynote. Mr. Hawthorn went to the stage to introduce Lloyd. Following Mr. Hawthorn's introduction, a crowd warmer would come out and get the energy level up.

The floor was vibrating from the jumping, the walls were ringing from the bass of the music playing, and the audience was clapping and yelling Lloyd's catchphrase DOGWA. Lloyd was standing still while he meditated trying to calm his nervous energy. He reminisced over his years on the road and those conversations with Scott and the friendship that became the better parts of his life. Lloyd grabbed his back which was sore from the previous day. "Ouch," he said out loud as he stretched.

"Can we get you something?" asked an attendant.

"No, I'm just sore from a little sprain in my back. Did you see that crowd yesterday? I heard today's is even bigger. Remind me not to jump so much on the stage today before

I start my speech." Everyone on Lloyd's Team laughed. They all knew he couldn't stop himself.

"Lloyd, it's your time to take the stage," Liz said. "This is the big one. Go get 'em!" She gave him a good luck kiss on the cheek.

Lloyd appeared on the stage. The crowd got even louder as he came out jumping up and down keeping the energy up. After a few more minutes, the music was slowly lowered so Lloyd could begin speaking. "Thank you all….thank you... thank you…" The crowd slowly settled as Lloyd made the hand motions to be seated. "Wow! What an entrance! What a crowd! Today, ladies and gentlemen, is a day for turning. A day for change. A day for DOGWA--Doing Only God's Will Always. Now we, the Team, picked that for a reason. If you turn it around it says Aw God. Like Aw God, really? Do I have to today? The answer is yes, but it's up to you. Do you have the discipline? Discipline will be the key to success or failure in life. Really. Let's look at it from a different angle: Everyone should be brushing their teeth, right? It's a daily discipline, but not having the discipline in your life to brush your teeth will lead you to eventually not having any teeth to brush. It's a success to keep your teeth clean. Just the same as reaching any other goals you have." The crowd roared with laughter at the analogy.

"So today I want to discuss something that will change the way you think about everything you do in your daily life. There was a time not long ago that I didn't have a purpose. I went through every single day the same as the day before. I'm sure many of you do that as well. It's okay, but it's not okay. Purpose is the cornerstone to getting the life you really want. A life that is lived not repeated like a series of video loops. Purpose is the driving force, the engine propelling the rest of you forward. I didn't have faith in God or myself. I met a friend during a very tragic time in my life. I didn't know anything about him or what was about to happen to me. What I did know is that I was pretty lost in the world and clung to my job for my identity.

"Today I want to present to you my ten keys for faithful living. These ten keys can bless you no matter what is happening in your life.

1. My life is a message. I will make it what I want it to be.
2. I take responsibility for who I am. I am responsible for my past and my future. I choose to live in the present.

3. I am a person of action. I choose to seize the moment, and I choose now.

4. My life is about loving and helping people. I have a caring and decided heart.

5. I make people and things flourish by the amount of time and care I give them.

6. I choose to have a great attitude. I am a happy person, and I will have a positive attitude towards others.

7. I know where I want my life to go. I have chosen my path to follow daily.

8. I will greet every day with a forgiving spirit. I will forgive myself and others.

9. My best preparation to live a good tomorrow is to live a great today.

10. I am a person of great faith. I believe all my talents and gifts come from my God.

"Those are all easy to do, aren't they? No, they sure aren't. If they were easy, you wouldn't need a list, right? We would all do them without thought."

Lloyd reached into the pocket of his suit jacket and withdrew a folded piece of paper. Holding it high enough for the camera to zoom in and rebroadcast his actions on the giant screen behind him, he unfolded it carefully. "This is a paper that my friend gave to me. Everything comes down to purpose. Please take a moment to read what it says."

Pausing his speech to give the audience time to read, he began again. "Without purpose in your life, no matter what it is, why even do it? Purpose gives us reason. Reason gives us goals. Goals give us momentum, and momentum drives your dream. Being faithful to your Creator and recognizing that all of your gifts and talents come from God give you a path to follow. If you allow God to speak to you in both your professional and personal life about how to most wisely use your gifts and talents to the best of your ability, you will have unlimited success in your life."

Lloyd finished the speech by recounting all the tragic steps that he had walked. He announced that he would be signing books in the lobby. He left the stage to a standing ovation from a crowd hungry for more.

Lloyd was seated at the book-signing table as the line formed. One by one seminar attendees brought his book *Faithful Living in a Faithless World* for his autograph. One book found its way in front of Lloyd as its owner stood looming over it. "Hey, Lloyd," came a voice like a ghost from his past. Lloyd looked up and confirmed it wasn't a ghost, but it was from his past.

"How should I address this, Ryan?"

"Could you please sign it with a special message? Would you please write 'From: The guy that changed his life.' and make it out 'To: The guy that got his life changed because someone else changed their life first'"? Lloyd looked up at Ryan. "I tried for a year to ignore this book after it was released, but I eventually bought a copy. I read it recently for the first time, then I read it a second time, and finally, after I read it the third time, I felt my heart change. I was a crying mess on the floor for about an hour. Lloyd, you changed my life with your experience. I'm so sorry I caused you all that pain."

"Truly, Ryan, it was a blessing. It was all part of God's plan. Without that tragedy I wouldn't...we Liz, Scott, and myself wouldn't be able to help as many people as we do."

"Thank you for your forgiveness. I know that could not have been easy to do."

"You're right, Ryan. It wasn't easy, but I had to do it. I hope you have forgiven everyone as well."

"I have. Like I said you changed my life. I will move on. It looks like you have a long line. It was good to see you. DOGWA, Brother."

"Likewise, Ryan. Take care of yourself." Ryan turned and walked away from the table. Lloyd took a moment to appreciate the completion of a long, sought-after goal which was to reach and change a heart as hard as Ryan's. "Now I have the momentum to change the world from faithless to faithful," he quietly said to himself. "Next, please. How may I sign your book?"

Part 2

10 DAILY ACTIONS TO FAITHFUL LIVING

I hope you enjoyed this story. I realized when the manuscript was complete, it left you hanging with this question: How do I apply this to my life. After consulting with my team, we realized I needed to write a section about implementing each action into your daily life.

After reading each section I recommend journaling about how you need to apply this to your life. You are not looking for perfection. You are taking inventory about how you need to apply this in your life. Remember: All actions do not have to be implemented at the same time.

Take a deep breath and enjoy the ride of your life. It's about the journey not the destination.

Enjoy your journey!

ACTION I

My life is a message. I will make it what I want it to be.

"Where there is no vision, the people perish..."
Proverbs 29:18

We need to dream about how our life will look. Who do you want to be? What do you want to achieve? When you pass away, what do you want your family and friends to say about you? I know that is hard to fathom, but we must use our emotions to move our actions. Let's think about it another way: It's your 80th birthday, and you are celebrating with your family and friends. Imagine the setting, and visualize who is in attendance. Do you see each person that is important to you and plays a key role in your life? If they were to stand up and say a few words about you and what you have meant to them, what would they say?

We must live our life with a message each day. Too many people live their life by the clock and not by a compass. The correlation is simple: The clock is about time; the compass is about direction. Do you live by time or direction? Are you so busy completing tasks that each day is a race? If you live by direction, what guides you? Do you listen for God's voice to direct you? Do you journal each day? Do you have a vision and mission statement that helps guide your message and actions? Think back to when you were a child: Do you remember the big DREAMS you had for your life? As adults we tend to stop dreaming or suppress our dreams. I want you to open your mind to BELIEVE you can still achieve your dreams, no matter how old you are or what has happened in your life. Say this: 1. I can and will achieve my dreams. 2. I can and will achieve my dreams. 3. I can and will achieve my dreams.

Reading this book means you are willing to acquire wisdom which helps mold our learning, experiences, and growth. We grow each day by increasing our knowledge in areas such as education, leadership, faith, health, and relationships. As we attain wisdom, our knowledge grows and allows us to learn the skills we need to help guide us in becoming the person we desire to be. Wisdom allows us to discover our passions which give us the energy, connections, and influence necessary to get greater daily results.

The reason we need to have a goal and plan for our life is so we may live by purpose, not by default. A speaker once asked his audience how many had a life insurance policy. Most of the room raised their hand. Then the speaker asked how many had a mission statement. Very few raised their hand. The speaker asked, "Why are you more prepared to die than to live?" I strongly believe you get in life what you create. Your thought processes and the conversations in your head are the base of the results you create in life. If you write out your goals, you are more likely to achieve them. Your mind is like an empty glass: It will hold everything you put into it. The brain has a subconscious part that is very powerful. Do you feed your mind with positive or negative self-talk? Positive self-talk will allow you to accomplish your goals and dreams. Being proactive in your words and actions is not by accident, but by design and the choices we make each day. Our mind is like a garden: The more you plant, water and fertilize, the more you will reap. Remember: Your thinking process will drive your expectations, and this will drive the message of your life.

Sam Walton once said, "High expectations are the key to everything." So why not have high expectations for your life? Remember the first daily action: "My life is a message. I will make it what I want it to be." YOU are in the driver's seat. Start planning today to make the life you want to achieve.

TAKE ACTION SUGGESTIONS:

1. Journal for 5 minutes per day. Ask yourself: What is my message? What do I want it to be?

2. Create your vison statement using the Vision Statement Builder*.

3. Write out your 80th birthday celebration. Who will attend? What will they say about your impact on their life?

"Living your life by design allows you not to live by default."
Gary Wilbers

*Begin your Take Action Suggestions by downloading your free resources at Resources.CultivatePositiveCulture.com

SCAN ME

ACTION II

I take responsibility for who I am. I choose to live in the present. I am responsible for my past and future.

"Consider this: Whoever sows sparingly will also reap sparingly, and whoever sows bountifully will also reap bountifully."
2 Corinthians 9:6

The key to living this message is to realize YOU are responsible for your life. Your life is not dependent on your childhood, family, parents, or even your past events. Think about it: Everything in your life exists because you first made a CHOICE about something.

Choices are the root of your results. Each choice starts with a behavior that overtime becomes a habit. Our choices either benefit or create consequences in our life.

The challenge is what we do with the choices we make. The idea of personal responsibility can completely change your life. The question is: What percentage of responsibility do you have in making any relationship in your life work?

A. 50/50   B. 51/49

C. 80/20   D. 100/0

The correct answer is 100/0. You have to be willing to give 100 percent with zero expectations of receiving anything in return. I know this is not easy in our society of instant gratification. I admit it is challenging, but anything worthwhile has a price. We have a tendency to play victim, blame, or expect someone else to solve our problems. When you realize that YOU ARE 100% PERCENT IN CONTROL OF YOURSELF, you will hit the jackpot of unlimited power for controlling your destiny. This is an empowering mindset to change in your life.

You must be willing to create, develop, and execute disciplines if you are truly going to take responsibility for becoming the person you want to be. Leave the blame game in the past. Stop using phrases such as I would have, I could have, and If only. These are the beginning of negative thoughts and actions. How do you do this? By using The High Achiever Mindset, which uses four practices: ENERGY, CONNECTIONS, INFLUENCE, and INTEGRATION that you can implement daily for taking responsibility for who you are.

ENERGY is the first practice you must learn to develop and produce each day. As you create daily disciplines, you create energy. Energy comes internally and externally from your actions. Each discipline feeds from the one before allowing you to gain momentum or energy with each practice. Energy is necessary to accomplish your goals and helps you take responsibility for not only the past but also the present. Once you recognize the areas of life you need to practice for gaining greater energy, you can start the discipline to take responsibility for harnessing the energy necessary to succeed.

The second practice is to create CONNECTIONS which are necessary for helping you achieve what you want to accomplish. Daily interaction with those you love and care about will strengthen your connection with them. As you strengthen your relationships, you will be offered new opportunities to make additional connections.

INFLUENCE is the third practice. By helping others achieve what they want in life through leadership, they in turn will help you achieve what you want in yours. The High Achiever Mindset believes the more you help others, the more abundance you will receive. It is not only about leadership but also your thoughts, words, and actions. An example I have illustrated hundreds of times is asking a big, strong man to volunteer. When I get him in front of the audience, I challenge him by saying that I have been lifting weights and ask if he can stop me from pushing his arms down when they are straight out to his side. (One of our greatest strengths is when we hold our arms straight out to our sides.) I then ask for another volunteer. I tell that volunteer I need him to say negative things about the other person. I remind the volunteers at least three times that these are false statements. The second volunteer has less than 30 seconds to say these false statements. I then ask the first volunteer to hold out his arms again. I can easily push them down. Why? It is because our subconscious mind cannot block false or negative statements. I then ask the second volunteer to say things he likes about the other person. I ask the first volunteer once again to hold out his arms. About 80-to-90% of the strength is back. This example shows the power of our mindset. If we feed ourselves with positive thoughts and understand we are responsible for our actions, we will live more in the present and stop living in the past. We can't change the past, but we can change the future.

INTEGRATION is the last practice we must incorporate to make the changes we need for creating positive habits and disciplines. I hear people say they cannot change this or that.

I do not believe this because we can make the change if we are willing to make a choice to change. You can choose to change things in your life right now. For example, A New Year's resolution for a lot of people is to lose weight. Why do most not succeed? They declare they want to make a change, but they do not commit to this. A commitment to lose weight looks like this:

1. Write the change down and make it a SMART goal.
2. Decide what habits/disciplines you need to make it happen.
3. Commit to the new habits/disciplines.
4. Find an accountability partner.
5. Declare your intention publicly.

If you create a habit/discipline and are held accountable, you will achieve your goal.

As you start using the areas of ENERGY, CONNECTIONS, INFLUENCE and INTEGRATION, you will be responsible for yourself, and you will create more abundance in the lives of others. God seems to always share abundance with those who help others because He wants us to be a servant leader. God gives us the power to achieve what we believe we can achieve. Remember: Responsibility is the key to your success. Are you willing to be responsible for creating the success you want in life? The greatest reward is to reach the top of your mountain and be able to share that magnificent view with those closest to you.

TAKE ACTION SUGGESTIONS:

1. Journal for 5 minutes per day. Ask yourself: What new habits do I need to create in my life?

2. Pick one habit you will start today and use the Habit Maker* to track your accountability.

3. Think of 5 relationships both professionally and personally that are most important to you. Fill out the Relationship Builder Form*.

"It's your life. Why not live the life you want to live?"
Gary Wilbers

*Begin your Take Action Suggestions by downloading your free resources at Resources.CultivatePositiveCulture.com

SCAN ME

ACTION III
I am a person of action.
I choose to seize the moment and I choose NOW!

"Faith is the realization of what is hoped for and evidence of the things not seen."
Hebrews 11:1

Two words we need to consider each day in our lives are THINK and ACTION. Self-belief is one of the most convincing characteristics we need to have before we can become the success we want. We must find the belief that we can and will accomplish anything we set our minds to achieve.

Self-belief is the thinking of and acting on what we want to accomplish. It's the conduit between your attitude and willpower to succeed. As you create what you want to accomplish, you must feed your thoughts with positive reinforcement so you can and will achieve what you want. As you reflect on where you want to go, do the following exercise to determine the action you will take going forward:

The first thing you need to do is grab a pen and paper. The first part of the process is to acknowledge and appreciate where you are right now. Looking back at the last 12-36 months, write out your responses to these questions:

1. What did I accomplish?

2. What were my biggest disappointments?

After you have honestly answered these questions, reflect about what you have learned in these areas. These life lessons will help you see where you need to put your action and efforts going forward. Spend some time answering the third question:

3. What did I learn?

These three questions are helping you form what you need to do in the future. When you have a positive internal focus for increasing your results, it gives you the momentum to succeed. It starts to create a transformation in the conscious part of your brain to empower you to succeed. You are taking action in creating your world instead of letting circumstances dictate your success. Next answer these questions:

4. How do I limit myself? In which areas of my life am I not achieving what I want? What do I say about myself to explain these failures?

This is a very important reflection point because these questions and answers will give you insight about what is stopping you from taking action to create what you want. Try not to overanalyze the why. Just let your conscious mind help you in answering each question. This will allow you to be true to who you really are.

Finally, download the resource to determine your values. Write out a clarifying statement for each value you choose (normally three-to-five values at the most). It is vital to really decide what is most important in your life. What are the hidden beliefs behind who you are and who you want to be? What values do you demonstrate each day? When we identify our personal values, it provides the strongest motivation for change and achieving what we want most in life. These personal values should be the words that are most central to our life such as integrity, honesty, compassion, keeping promises, loving, caring, etc.

5. Write your personal values and then review them.

Write a clarifying statement for each value.

When we take the time to clarify our values, we can see ourselves "living" those values. We take action in making them an integral part of our daily living. I believe writing a clarifying statement for each value gives us a verbal picture, vision, or target to help us understand what to do for achieving that guiding value in our life.

The discipline of choosing is the key to taking action each day. As we choose our direction in these areas of body, mind, spirit and heart, we will start following that path. The discipline we create in our life through deliberate, focused choices will determine our results. As we create disciplines, they become habits. As they become habits, they become daily routines that allow us to grow and become the person we choose to be.

Nobody does all these things every day, but the people who make a habit of improving themselves every day are taking ACTION for their lives. Remember to set goals for yourself in these areas: business, financial, health, mental, family, spiritual, lifestyle, and relationships. Take time to write down your goals. If you write down your goals, you increase your odds of achieving them. If you want to achieve something, start today. Action only happens when you choose to make it happen. Are you ready to take ACTION?

TAKE ACTION SUGGESTIONS:

1. Journal for 5 minutes per day. Ask yourself: What action do I want to take in my life?

2. Write out your answers to these questions:

   a. What did I accomplish?

   b. What were my biggest disappointments?

   c. What did I learn?

   d. How do I limit myself? In which areas of my life am I not achieving what I want? What do I say about myself to explain these failures?

   e. What are my personal values? Write a clarifying statement for each value?

3. Fill out Clarifying Your Values* worksheet. Start establishing your goals using The Yearly Target* worksheet.

*"Life is not about living in mediocrity;
life is about living in our future self."*
Gary Wilbers

*Begin your Take Action Suggestions by downloading your free resources at Resources.CultivatePositiveCulture.com

SCAN ME

ACTION IV

My life is about loving and helping people.
I have a caring and decided heart.

"Whoever is without love does not know God, for God is love."
1 John 4:8

As we look at the actions for faithful living, we must examine our personal identity by asking the question: Who am I? As we examine ourselves emotionally, spiritually, physically and mentally, we begin to understand our true identity. Self-examination allows us to recognize our strengths, weaknesses, and unique passions. Take time and identify the roles you play: husband, mother, father, boss, son, daughter, leader, friend, spiritual leader, etc. When we identify the roles we play and clarify how we want to live these roles, we start to understand who we are in all areas of our life. As we progress in life, we sometimes forget the people that are closest to us and how much they mean to us.

We are always searching to find our purpose. If I asked you what is your unique ability, how would you respond? Unique ability is the essence of what you love to do and what you do best. There are four characteristics of unique ability:

1. It's a superior ability that other people notice and value. You are passionate about using it and want to use it as much as possible.
2. It's energizing both for you and others.
3. There's a sense of never-ending improvement. You keep getting better and never run out of possibilities for growth.
4. Because your unique ability is fueled by tremendous passion, it can be a very powerful force and create enormous value for you and others.

When you combine talent and passion, you have a recipe for never-ending improvement, energy, excitement, and higher levels of achievement.

Your unique ability is very powerful for your continued growth as an individual. My unique ability is motivating others to find their true passion and helping them find what matters. Over the last several years I have had the pleasure of working more with my unique ability within my own life. I have helped others find their unique ability by coaching them to find their passion, skills, and drive. I am also able to share this message through books, speeches, and trainings.

I feel my unique ability is motivating others to find their direction for reaching high performance in every area of life.

How do you discover your unique ability? Unique ability shapes how you show up in your way of being. It's the YOU that makes you who you are. Your unique ability is your:

- Skills
- Talents
- Characteristics
- Activities
- Creativity
- Habits

These are some of the means by which it can be expressed, yet it's more than any of these. It's also an expression of your values. Remember in ACTION III, you wrote your personal values and clarifying statement. These values will help you identify your unique ability. Have you ever felt the excitement of doing something you excel at and others praise you for it? You have experienced your unique ability in action. You use it so naturally and willingly that it's constantly evolving and improving as you move through life. When you give it room and focus, evolution speeds up the value you create for others and yourself. My hope is you will find your unique ability because when you do, it will drive you to love, care, and help people.

Here are three areas for you to think about as you love, care, and help others with a decided heart:

1. The Power of Love: Love is not always exactly the way we think. In our relationships we have to show love through actions and not just emotions. How do we show others we care? Are we supportive when needed? Do we offer guidance to the people in our life? Do we take time to mentor what we expect? Showing our love comes in many forms, but we must be willing to help and care for others.

2. The Power of Why: Friedrich Nietzsche said, "If you know the why, you can live any how." Give some thoughts to why you are doing what you are doing in your relationships with your spouse, children, family, co-workers, etc. When we understand our why, we are more apt to live as the person we want to be. It allows us to discover the how because it gives us the fuel to overcome our challenges and adversities. It is powerful to understand our why spiritually, emotionally, physically, and mentally.

3. The Power of You: Ask yourself this question: What more can I do? This question is related to every area of our life. If I want better relationships in my life, what more can I do to show my love? If I want to be a better coworker for my company, what more can I do to show I am a leader who will get better each day? If I want to get in shape physically, what more can I do to exercise and eat a healthy diet? If I want to improve my financial condition, what can I do to budget and learn new ways of handling my money? If I want to improve spiritually, what more can I do to take time for daily prayers and meditation? In every area of your life, ask yourself what more can I do? If you take time to answer these questions, you will be starting on the path to fulfilling the purpose that God has chosen for you. It won't be easy to make the changes, but if you make a commitment to discipline yourself, you will create a routine that becomes a habit.

TAKE ACTIONS SUGGESTIONS:

1. Journal for 5 minutes per day. Ask yourself: What more can I do?

2. Decide which 5-to-7 roles are most important to you and write a clarifying statement for each role using the Life Roles Builder*.

3. Take time to discover your unique ability by filling out the Unique Ability Creator*.

> *"Finding your purpose is God's gift to you.*
> *Sharing your purpose is your gift to God."*
>
> Gary Wilbers

*Begin your Take Action Suggestions by downloading your free resources at Resources.CultivatePositiveCulture.com

SCAN ME

ACTION V

I make people and things flourish by the amount of time and care I give to them.

*"For whoever wishes to save his life will lose it,
but whoever loses his life for my sake will find it."*
Matthew 16:25

One morning on my way to the office, I heard the radio announcer say that scientists have recently discovered that they believe the world should operate on a twenty-five-hour cycle versus the twenty-four hours we operate on currently. What would you do if you had an extra hour each day? Don't answer sleep. How about exercise, work, study, read, spend time with family, learn a new skill or hobby, or spend time with your friends?

No, we are not going to get an extra hour in our day, but do we spend our current time on truly the most important things in our life? We must ask ourselves how will I spend my time in my life?

In the earlier actions we discussed vision, habits, values, goals, roles, and unique ability in order to know our direction. We must create a personal mission statement that becomes our written proclamation of who we are and what we're about. It should express the contributions you want to make, the things you want to do, and the kind of person you want to be. It becomes your compass helping you calibrate when you get off course. It becomes a reminder of what is most important in your life. Your personal mission statement is an affirmation of your highest priorities which you have determined by your roles and values. It is your DASH, the little mark between the date you were born and the date when you leave this earth. What will your DASH be?

My goal is to motivate you to create your very own personal mission statement. I would like to share with you my personal mission statement to give you a better understanding and also to give you encouragement for writing your own mission statement. If you already have a mission statement, review it and see if it still represents your vision, values, and roles.

My mission statement is "My God is the path I will follow. My family is my number one priority to care for and love. The person I am is made by my integrity as a person. I am a creative individual always looking for ways to be innovative in my life and career. My health and fitness gives me the strength to prepare for the daily challenges of life.

I will always share my talents and knowledge with others."
7/17/06

Since I have determined my highest priorities, I have spent more time in the areas mentioned in my personal mission statement. Do I get off track at times? Yes. I review my mission statement each week which allows me to calibrate my compass. I am not perfect in each of these areas, but knowing my direction and where I am going helps me stay on the right path. Before I wrote out my mission statement, I was going down the wrong path. I thought if I was growing my business to be successful, that would take care of our issues because financially we would not have to worry. I thought that if I am a success, my closest relationships would understand that I cared for them. I was not giving the people closest to me my time. They felt as though I did not care about them. I am a lucky man because my spouse was so understanding, and my children were very young during this time. We need to express our love through our time, care, and actions. I thank God each day for pointing me in the right direction. In 2006 I was lost, but now I follow God each day.

My final message to you about this action is to spend time with the people who are important in your life. Each day show these people how much you love and care for them. Time is a gift from God. Remember to use each day, hour, and minute wisely. We all get the same twenty-four hours each day, but what you do with your twenty-four hours determines if you are living your life by design.

TAKE ACTIONS SUGGESTIONS:

1. Journal for 5 minutes per day. Ask yourself: What is my mission in life?
2. Create a draft of your mission statement using the Mission Builder*. Review your mission statement each week for calibration.
3. Share your mission statement draft with someone you love. Have that person hold you accountable.

> *"Everyone thinks of changing the world,*
> *but no one thinks of changing himself."*
> Leo Tolstoy

*Begin your Take Action Suggestions by downloading your free resources at Resources.CultivatePositiveCulture.com

SCAN ME

ACTION VI

I choose to have a great attitude. I am a happy person and I will have a positive attitude towards others.

"A joyful heart is the health of the body,
but a depressed spirit dries up the bones."
Proverbs 17:22

A positive attitude is approaching life with optimism and confidence. Developing a positive attitude requires replacing negative thinking with positive thoughts in an effort to create a successful outlook. Many people want to have a positive attitude, but they go about getting it in the wrong manner. How do you get a positive attitude?

Let's analyze the definition in order to get a better understanding about how you can implement a positive attitude into your daily life. The first part talks about approaching life with optimism and confidence. You must first decide to create a habit of implementing a positive mentality into your daily actions. This is the hard part because it must become a habit to make it a reality. Optimism and confidence are emotions controlled by your brain. However, it must be a conditioned response not just a feeling.

The next part of the definition is replacing negative thinking with positive thinking. The key point that you must change is how you look at things. The way you view information will determine your result of negative or positive thinking. Charles Swindoll said, "Life is 10% what happens to us and 90% how we react to it." Think about that. When something happens, do you go towards the negative, or do you see the positive side of the situation?

The last part of the definition is creating a successful outlook. This is done by knowing your compass (direction) and purpose. One of the reasons I wrote this book is for you to think about what your purpose is and how you can discover it. Spend time reflecting and journaling about this. As you spend time learning, growing and experiencing, you will see your outlook become more positive and grateful because you will understand that the little things you do each day are making a difference in the world.

To become a positive person, implement these four strategies:
- Showing gratitude daily
- Read and listen to motivational material
- Journaling

• Exercise

Gratitude is giving or appreciating something or someone for a contribution they make to you or your team. Jon Gordon, an American author and speaker on the topics of leadership, culture, sales and teamwork, said that you can't be blessed and stressed at the same time. Each day show your gratitude to the people you interact with such as your spouse, co-workers, boss, children, etc. When you show gratitude through your actions, relationships will be more positive.

The second strategy is to read and listen to motivational material such as this book and podcasts. Turn off the negative media and input positive messages that will help you become the person you want to be. Our media is appealing to our emotions to illicit the negative. The more we feed our mind with positive messages, the more our mind will change. Zig Ziglar, one of the greatest motivators of all time, said, "People often say that motivation doesn't last. Well, neither does bathing—that's why we recommend it daily." Remember: The more we plant, fertilize and water our mind, the more it will grow.

The third strategy is journaling. At least once a day write out your thoughts. This allows you to acknowledge what is on your mind. You may not know what to journal about. I start with what I am grateful for today. I then ask myself a question and answer it. This allows my mind to experience where I am at that moment. Remember: The analogy of the compass helps give you direction. If you cannot see yourself journaling each day, journal once per week. To start a habit begin in bite-size chunks and build on that. The goal is to start the journey of journaling. Don't worry about perfection.

The last strategy is exercise. It is proven that exercise will help you in every area of your life. Exercise provides you with a more positive attitude because of the energy it gives your mind and body. I believe exercise in any form allows us to create the energy we need each day, week, and month for accomplishing our goals. Spend 30 minutes three-to-five times per week exercising. It can be walking, running, cardio, weights, biking, group classes, etc. You decide. The key is to start exercising weekly. I know some of you are thinking that you don't have time. Do you realize that it is only 2-to-2.5 hours per week out of the 168 hours we get each week? To accomplish this habit, you must make it a priority. The average person spends 2 hours and 22 minutes per day on social media and messaging platforms. If you cut out thirty minutes of the time you spend on social media, you will have time to exercise. Remember: We must be willing to put CHARGE (Create Habits Around Real Goals Everyday) into our life. When you start being proactive in creating a positive attitude, you will like the rewards of your efforts.

TAKE ACTION SUGGESTIONS:

1. Journal for 5 minutes per day. Ask yourself: What am I grateful for today?
2. Pick 3 podcasts to listen to each week. (Check out my podcast at Chargepodcast.com)
3. Start a simple energy and lifestyle program using the High Achievers Energy Checklist*.

*"Give yourself permission to CHARGE each day
to become the person you were meant to be."*
Gary Wilbers

*Begin your Take Action Suggestions by downloading your free resources at Resources.CultivatePositiveCulture.com

SCAN ME

ACTION VII

I know where I want my life to go.
I have chosen my path to follow daily.

"For I know the plans I have for you, says the Lord, plans for welfare and not for evil, to give you a future and a hope."
Jeremiah 29:11

Have you ever noticed how easily people with a positive attitude can influence you? Influence is not power; it is more of a sharing of wisdom and knowledge. To gain a high achiever mindset we have to recognize the wisdom within ourselves and realize we can and should influence ourselves each day. We grow as a leader through our daily actions and words. Our goal is not having power over others but rather having a discipline over our thoughts, words, and actions. This allows us to become influential in who we want to be and what we want to accomplish each day.

True leaders lead themselves before they ever try to influence others. This action is designed to create a self-discipline enabling us to influence others and share ourselves with the community of people we impact. As we grow in our faith, we empower ourselves to be better in all of our relationships. Why? Because when God is our center, we develop greater clarity of understanding ourselves. God then helps us see the ways we need to grow in our relationships. When we take action to influence our own life, we will start influencing others. To truly know where we want to go in life, we must slow down long enough to ponder these questions: What direction do I need to follow? How can I fulfill what God has set out for me to accomplish if I don't spend time in prayer and meditation? Each day seek what God has in store for you by being open, honest, and vulnerable. Spend some time reflecting in prayer. It is hard to follow God's will and not your own. We all must dedicate our work to be used for God's purposes and not ours. When we allow God to bless us, we are open to Him.

Rick Warren, author of *A Purpose Driven Life*, wrote in a devotional how he defined dedicating your works with the word SUCCEED:

Start working enthusiastically.

Understand who you really work for.

Concentrate on building your character.

Care about the people you work with.

Exceed what is expected of you.

Expand your skills to SUCCEED at work.

Dedicate your work to be for God's purpose.

God wants us to succeed in life. He wants us to succeed spiritually, but He also wants us to succeed in our work. God wants us to be a witness at work which allows us to use our platform for the glory of God.

I believe once we know where we want our life to go, then it is about choosing a path to follow daily. It is vital to set goals because this becomes our roadmap to success for reaching our destination. Each year I take time to set goals in areas such as health, spiritual, relationships, career, education, self, and family. This becomes a written plan for keeping me on track to achieve the goals I have set.

What is a goal? It is an object to be reached or attained. If you want to reach or attain a goal, you must first know what your goal is. Multiple studies have shown that writing out your goals increases your chances of achieving them. The key is to make it a SMART goal: Specific, Measurable, Attainable, Realistic and Timebound. Your brain agrees with what you want to accomplish. Writing your goals about what you want to achieve makes them real in your mind. I also believe you need to post your goals in a very visible place for daily review. This gives a clear reminder about the path you want to follow.

The next step in goal setting is to break your goals into action steps. You must have a method for achieving your goals. If you break your goals down into actionable steps, you will achieve them. Here is the method I use: First, create the goal you want to achieve by using the SMART method. For example, I will lose 25 lbs. by December 31st. Does it meet all areas of the SMART method? (Specific=Yes, Measurable=Yes, Attainable=Yes, Realistic=Yes, Timebound=Yes.) Take that yearly goal and break it into a 90-day action plan. Then create a 30-day action plan for ways to achieve the goal in smaller increments: 1. Every Monday weigh and track my progress on a chart. 2. Exercise 4 times per week for a minimum of 30 minutes each. 3. Using the daily tracking guide log what you eat. 4. Always take the stairs versus the elevator. 5. Check in with an accountability partner, share the weekly plan, and review last week's plan. Committing to these smaller steps makes the goal of losing 25 lbs. even easier.

The last step is committing and disciplining yourself so that you can achieve the goal. I am a firm believer that you must put your goal in a visible place for reviewing daily in order to follow the path you have chosen. A goal is always a challenge to achieve. If you have the commitment and discipline to follow your chosen path, you will see great rewards for your efforts. Take ACTION for achieving your goals.

TAKE ACTION SUGGESTIONS:

1. Journal for 5 minutes per day. Ask yourself: Where does God want my life to go? What goals should I take action to achieve?

2. Use The Yearly Target* to finalize your goal setting plan.

> *"GOALS: It's like having your headlights on because you know where you are going."*
> Gary Wilbers

*Begin your Take Action Suggestions by downloading your free resources at Resources.CultivatePositiveCulture.com

SCAN ME

ACTION VIII

I will greet every day with a forgiving spirit.
I will forgive myself and others.

*"Then Peter approaching asked him,
'Lord, if my brother sins against me, how often must
I forgive him? As many as seven times?'
Jesus answered, 'I say to you, not seven times
but seventy-seven times.' "*
Matthew 18:21-22

The eighth action is one of the most challenging because our pride and ego get in the way. Over the years I have struggled with this action. I am a very strong-willed individual, so forgiving is not one of my strengths. Anyone who knows me well would agree with that statement, especially my wife. Through the years I have been more proactive in having a forgiving spirit. I have realized during my prayer and reflection time each morning that I need to spend time in thought which allows me to understand my weakness in this area. In reflecting over my previous day, I realized that if I am not willing to forgive myself, I am not ready to forgive others.

In the above Bible verse Jesus makes it clear that forgiveness is not easy. Living in a state of forgiveness is not a one-time choice; it's a daily choice. We must be willing to forgive ourselves and others. Forgiveness normally requires a lifetime of forgiving, but it is one of the actions that makes us the person God means for us to be. We must open our hearts and minds to understand how our forgiveness cannot only change us but also the people we forgive. Too often people see forgiveness as a weakness; instead it is a sign of strength. The key thing we must remember is that forgiveness comes from the heart. The emotion of true forgiveness heals us.

Forgiveness is the action or process of forgiving or being forgiven. Consider this scenario: A drunk driver hits your family car as you are coming back from your parents' house during Christmas. Everyone in the vehicle is injured, but your son or daughter is killed. How would you respond? Could you forgive this person? I ultimately cannot answer these questions because it has not happened to me or my family. I hope over time I could forgive this person, but I know it would not be from my strength but from God helping me see this person as a child of His. I know the only way I could forgive would be from the power of the Holy Spirit.

Reflecting each morning or evening allows us the space to give thought to our words and actions. We are called daily to spend some time with our Lord so we may think and hear His message. The norm in our society is to be busy all the time making this a real challenge because we have so many distractions keeping us from spending reflective time each day. Do you spend time each day watching tv? Do you spend time each day on social media? In *The Screwtape Letters* C.S. Lewis writes the story of a demon who is training his nephew how to handle humans. The demon writes, "Whatever their bodies do affects their souls. It is funny how mortals always picture us as putting things into their minds: in reality our best work is done by keeping things out..." As you can see, Satan doesn't have to do much to keep our minds away from God. All he has to do is distract us. If we allow the curse of busyness in our daily lives, it will not allow us time to think and reflect.

How we spend our time shows how we cultivate a positive culture in our life and the lives of others. Take an inventory of how you are spending your time. Recalibrate your focus in order to take action for spending time in reflection and prayer every day. I admit I don't take time for prayer and reflection every day, but I am working on it because I know the difference it makes in my life.

TAKE ACTION SUGGESTIONS:

1. Journal for 5 minutes per day. Ask yourself: Am I a forgiving person? How do I spend my time each day?
2. Create a Morning Magic Routine*. Check out the Resources site listed below for an example of a Morning Magic Routine.

"When you haven't forgiven those who have hurt you, you turn your back against your future. When you do forgive, you start walking forward."

Tyler Perry

*Begin your Take Action Suggestions by downloading your free resources at Resources.CultivatePositiveCulture.com

SCAN ME

ACTION IX

My best preparation to live a good tomorrow is to live a great today.

*"This is the day the Lord has made,
let us rejoice and be glad in it."*
Psalm 118:24

As you read this section, I want you to think about where your life will be ten years from today. This is what I call forward thinking, the ability to look ahead and visualize how a project, task, time frame, etc. looks after you have completed it.

If you were sitting here ten years from today and looking back over those years, what would have happened in your life, both personally and professionally, for you to feel happy with your progress? The challenge is balancing your personal and professional life. We tend to focus on only one aspect of our lives, but it is equally important to have a well-defined plan in both of these areas. To achieve great results in both areas, we must first have a plan and then set personal and professional goals. The High Achiever Mindset is about creating what you want to achieve. As we all know, life moves at a rapid pace. The challenge is not to look back and wonder where those years went. We do not know how many days we have, so live life to the fullest. Live your life looking ahead and not looking back. As we grow in our faith, we realize God should be the center of our life. Our faith centers life and provides clarity for our journey.

One area in our life that must be tackled for us to take actions for faithful living is discipline. Discipline as a noun is the practice of training people to obey rules or codes of behavior, using punishment to correct disobedience. This word can be used in both a positive and negative situation. Using parables Jesus tried to teach the disciples to follow the right path. God shared His teachings in the Bible so that we can comprehend how He wants us to be disciplined in our lives. I believe discipline is what makes the difference between a person who lives a purpose-driven life versus the person who just goes through life. Discipline influences us to make better decisions and choices each day. Discipline allows us to become the driver of our lives.

How does this apply to the ninth action? As you can see from the other actions, each one builds on the other. Momentum propels you to great days. We all know it is not easy to build momentum, but once you do, look out. Remember when you were a child playing on merry-go-rounds? A bunch of your friends would pile on, weighing the merry-go-round down. Those first steps of getting the merry-go-round started were the hardest. You had to push and pull, grimace and groan, and throw your whole body into the effort. One step, two steps, three steps--it seemed as though you were getting nowhere. After a long, hard effort you finally were able to get a little speed and run alongside it. Even though you were moving and your friends were cheering louder to get the speed they really wanted, you had to keep running faster and faster with all your might. At last you found success when you jumped on with your friends. You found the joy of the wind in your face and watched the world turn into a smear of colors. After a while the merry-go-round started to slow down. You'd hop off and run alongside for a minute to get the speed back up, or you could simply give it a couple of good pushes and hop back on. Once the merry-go-round was spinning at a good clip, momentum took over and made it easy to keep going.

This is the same process we go through to adopt change into our life. We start with small actions that create habits around real goals every day. (CHARGE) That allows us to achieve the results we want in life. The process is slow, but it is vital that we take action each day. The action helps us create a new habit which will create the momentum we need to cultivate the positive culture we want. The secret lies in the daily actions we take. This is different from what society shows us. Our society shows us the glamour and glitz of how easy it is for the superstars. The struggles along the way are left out. It takes daily actions for creating the discipline to form the habits needed to build the momentum that will propel your life forward. Once you establish the momentum in your life, nothing can stop you but yourself. Remember: Your best preparation to live a good tomorrow is to live a GREAT today.

I challenge you to give some thought to your forward thinking so you can find the success and results you are looking for. Remember: Live each day to the fullest. Make each day the best day of your life. It all starts with that first step.

TAKE ACTION SUGGESTIONS:

1. Journal for 5 minutes per day. Ask yourself: What will my life look like ten years from now? What do I want for my life?

2. Watch the video *Everybody Dies But Not Everybody Lives*. https://vimeo.com/163657401

3. Fill out the Forward Thinking Model*.

"Momentum is like a merry-go-round that starts very slowly. Based on our daily actions, the energy increases."
Gary Wilbers

*Begin your Take Action Suggestions by downloading your free resources at Resources.CultivatePositiveCulture.com

SCAN ME

ACTION X

I am a person of faith. I believe all my talents and gifts come from my God.

"Show me your ways, O Lord, teach me your paths; guide me in your truth and teach me, for you are God my savior, and my hope is in you all day long."
Psalm 25: 4-5

As I share my final action, I hope you have found some worthwhile actions for making your life what you want it to be. We all have the capability to make our life the BEST if we choose to take action. This action is about you sharing that you are a person of faith, and you believe your talents and gifts come from God.

I had a hard time with the fact that God was the reason for my success. One of the reasons I had this challenge was because I believed my hard work and abilities were the reason for my success. Fortunately, I have seen the light, and this has changed with age and wisdom. Realizing that my gifts and talents come from God has changed my relationship with Him. It made me start searching for my purpose in life. Using my Purpose Statement Creator, I have defined my purpose and try to live it each day.

My purpose statement is "The purpose of my life is to be a servant leader; to live fully energized with joy and presence so that I might inspire others to give, love and make a difference each day."

To really learn about our purpose, we must be willing to listen to God and hear the message He is sharing with us. Over the years I have reflected about the blessings God has poured into my life, career, business, finances, relationships, spouse, family, and health. I realized they all happened because of my God. At Sunday Mass recently the priest was talking about the decisions to use our God-given talents and gifts to become and do what we want. If we are willing to slow down, pause, and allow God to share His thoughts with us, we can permit those thoughts to enter our mind. Please take time to read Ephesians 1:3-14 in the Bible. You will read that we were chosen and destined in accord with the purpose of the One who accomplishes all things, so that we who first hoped in Christ might exist for the praise of His glory.

Recognizing that our gifts and talents are God-given helps us to overcome the challenges, obstacles, and roadblocks we face daily. The strongest leaders realize they need help to become their best. Achieving great results in your life is the opportunity to become the person God is calling you to be. One of the traits I believe you must have is the attitude of gratitude for acknowledging the good things in life. Dan Sullivan, founder and president of The Strategic Coach Inc, defines gratitude as "An internally-generated capability that allows an individual to create and discover unlimited meaning and value in every situation and relationship in life." Let's analyze this definition of gratitude:

Internally-generated capability: This means we have the ability within ourselves to generate this capability. Gratitude does not come from possessions. We have the drive to find gratitude in the smallest areas of our life. For example, the sunshine that warms the day.

Create unlimited meaning and value: Gratitude allows us to discover why we appreciate something. Everyone values different things. For example, for one person seeing the sunset is gratitude; for another it may just be another sunset. The challenge is to search yourself and find what holds gratitude in your life. Each day at the beginning and the end, write down at least three things that created meaning and value and that you are grateful for. Most people live life but forget to live their life.

As you make your list, it will be easy to identify the people closest to you such as spouse, children, parents, etc. You should show daily gratitude to these people through your words and actions. The more challenging areas are interactions with a co-worker, job issues, or someone you had an argument with. Include the relationship you have with your Creator. God provides the backbone for giving us the capability and willingness to open our heart and mind and allow Him to help us.

My prayer for you is that you take time to reflect, pray, and allow God to speak to you each day. You are created to be a person of God. Go out each day and seek the wisdom to find that person. Life is not a destination but a journey. Your journey starts with YOU. Blessings! Make it a GREAT day!

TAKE ACTION SUGGESTIONS:

1. Journal for 5 minutes per day. Ask yourself: What is my purpose? What am I grateful for today?

2. Create your purpose statement using the Purpose Statement Creator*.

3. Every morning and evening write in your journal 3 things you are grateful for that day.

"Your purpose defines you, guides you, and allows you to be the person God created you to be."

Gary Wilbers

*Begin your Take Action Suggestions by downloading your free resources at Resources.CultivatePositiveCulture.com

SCAN ME

Thank You

Thank you for reading *Cultivate Positive Culture: 10 Actions to Faithful Living*. I hope this book helps you on your journey to living a purposeful life. Use my mantra of CHARGE: Create Habits Around Real Goals Everyday. As I end this book, I want to share an expression I wrote using the 10 Actions to Faithful Living:

"My message makes me responsible to be a person of action. My life is about loving and helping people. I help them flourish by the amount of time and care I give to them. I choose to be a happy person, and I will have a positive attitude toward others. I have chosen my path to follow daily and will greet each day with a forgiving spirit. I will live a great life today because I am a person of faith, and I know my gifts come from my God."

I look forward to seeing you on your journey.

Blessings!

Make it a GREAT day!

Bibliography

"Charles R. Swindoll Quotes." Quotes.net. STANDS4 LLC, 2020. Web. 4 May 2020.

<https://www.quotes.net/quote/17859>

Gordon, Jon. "If You Are Feeling Blessed, You Will Not Feel Stressed." YouTube, Uploaded by Jon Gordon, 26 Sep. 2018, https://www.youtube.com/watch?v=DNavHDqiZ-w

«Leo Tolstoy Quotes.» Quotes.net. STANDS4 LLC, 2020. Web. 4 May 2020. <https://www.quotes.net/quote/18070>

Lewis, C S. The Screwtape Letters, 1943. Print.

Nietzsche, Friedrich Wilhelm, 1844-1900. Twilight Of the Idols, or, How to Philosophize with a Hammer. New York :Oxford University Press, 1998

"Sam Walton Quotes." Quotes.net. STANDS4 LLC, 2020. Web. 4 May 2020. <https://www.quotes.net/quote/18721>

Sullivan, Dan. The Gratitude Principle. Publisher, Strategic Coach, Incorporated, 1999

"Tyler Perry." AZQuotes.com Wind and Fly LTD, 2020. 04 May 2020.

https://www.azquotes.com/quote/531269

Warren, Rick, 1954-. The Purpose-Driven Life : What on Earth Am I Here for? Grand Rapids, Mich. :Zondervan, 2002.

"Zig Ziglar Quotes." Famous Quotes at BrainyQuote. Xplore Inc, 2020. 4 May 2020. Zig Ziglar Quotes.

About the Author

Gary Wilbers has been an entrepreneur and owner of multiple businesses in Missouri since 1990. He created an acronym that has shaped his life's foundation: CHARGE: Create Habits Around Real Goals Everyday. He studied entrepreneurs such as Sam Walton, Brendon Burchard, Brian Tracy and Charles Red Scott and learned their principles. Then he built his roadmap for personal success.

The first business Gary built, Mid-America Wireless, started as a small two-man company and culminated with ten regional storefronts and over one hundred and fifty employees. He developed a culture of learning and a sharing of knowledge within his companies. His goal and commitment were to always make a team member better equipped than when he/she started. Gary created a framework, The High Achiever Mindset, using his success as the foundation. He now shares his message as a keynote speaker, trainer, coach, and author in order to help others reach their goals, dreams, and ambitions. Gary is a certified High Performance Coach from the High Performance Institute. He has written three other publications.

Gary has been recognized by the Jefferson City Chamber with the Small Business of the Year Award in 1995 and the Chairman's Award in 2015. He was named one of the "Ten Outstanding Young Missourians" by the Missouri Junior Chamber of Commerce in 1996 and received the Jefferson City Jaycees Distinguished Service Award in 2000.

Gary is also involved in his community, giving his time and resources to several organizations. Gary served as the Campaign Co-Chair for the United Way of Central Missouri in 2001-2002 and as the Board Chairman in 2005. His passion is working with Special Olympics Missouri. He served on the Board for Special Olympics Missouri including serving as Board Chair and as the Capital Campaign Chair for the Training for Life Campus fund drive with the purpose of building a state-of-the-art facility for Missouri athletes. One of his greatest joys is playing unified golf with Keith Lueckenhoff, a SOMO athlete.

Gary and his wife Dana have three children: Chris, Adam and Elle and reside in Wardsville, MO.

GARY'S OTHER PUBLISHED WORKS

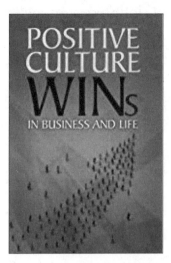

POSITIVE CULTURE WINS IN BUSINESS AND LIFE

Are you struggling with your career, family or even your health? Do toxic workplace experiences from the past haunt you and influence your every decision? You're not alone. Meet Johnny, Director of Sales with a Midwestern company. Johnny feels distant from his wife and kids and worries that his new job will be just as stressful as the last one. Under the guidance of a well-loved coach, he learns the "High Achiever Mindset" that forms the basis of the company's culture. Johnny finds out firsthand that Positive Culture Wins. Filled with practical strategies and an action plan for readers at every level, Positive Culture Wins is all about changing lives for the better. Filled with easy-to-apply strategies and a practical action plan, Johnny's story will show you firsthand that **POSITIVE CULTURE WINS.**

To purchase go to: goascend.biz/shop

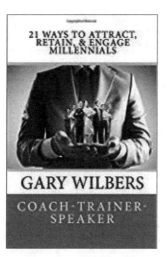

21 WAYS TO ATTRACT, RETAIN & ENGAGE MILLENNIALS

Organizations that effectively recruit and retain millennials will have a competitive advantage. You will learn the strategies you and your leaders need to help attract, retain, and engage millennials in your organization. Every generation is different but the key is how to harness their strengths in order to help them understand what is expected in the workforce. This book covers 7 strategies in each of the following areas:

- Attracting Millennials
- Retaining Millennials
- Engaging Millennials

To purchase go to: goascend.biz/shop

THE HIGH ACHIEVER LEADERSHIP FORMULA: 6 INGREDIENTS OF AN INSPIRING & INFLUENTIAL LEADER

Do you know what it takes to be a great leader in both your personal and professional life? The challenge is you become stuck in a never-ending cycle where your productivity suffers and the daily issues of life have you feeling mentally and emotionally exhausted. You feel uninspired as each new day becomes a merry-go-round where it seems like your world is spinning out of control. This isn't just another self-help book based on theory. As a successful entrepreneur and business owner for the last 25 years, Gary has taken this journey, made mistakes along the way, and come to the realization that every error made him better. Here is your opportunity to benefit from his experiences and shorten your learning curve.

The High Achiever Leadership Formula contains 6 ingredients of an inspiring and influential leader:

- The High Achiever Mindset
- The Leadership Time Solution
- The Leadership Communication Loop
- The Influence & Trust Builder
- The Conflict Resolution System
- The Strategic Organizational Playbook

To purchase go to: goascend.biz/shop

CONTACT GARY

Gary Wilbers is a speaker, author, coach and trainer who loves to help individuals and organizations cultivate a positive culture. Gary has been a successful entrepreneur for over 30 years and has realized the most important asset of any team is its people. Gary created a mantra of CHARGE: Create Habits Around Real Goals Everyday and shares his message with audiences who want to be inspired to take action in making changes that will enhance not only their professional life but also their personal life and the lives of others. Gary has studied the effects a positive culture makes in organizations and individuals for increasing performance. For more information on Keynote Speaking, Coaching and Training.

Contact Gary:

Speaking website: garywilbers.com

Coaching & Training website: goascend.biz

Phone: 573-644-6655

Email: gwilbers@goascend.biz

Ascend Business Strategies

1025 Southwest Blvd. Suite A

Jefferson City, MO 65109

To purchase bulk copies of this book at a discounted rate, please contact Dana Wilbers: dwilbers@goascend.biz or 574-644-6655